# SHAMANIC
## CHRISTIANITY

# SHAMANIC CHRISTIANITY

## THE DIRECT EXPERIENCE OF MYSTICAL COMMUNION

Bradford Keeney

Destiny Books
Rochester, Vermont

Destiny Books
One Park Street
Rochester, Vermont 05767
www.DestinyBooks.com

Destiny Books is a division of Inner Traditions International

LIBRARY OF CONGRESS CATALOGING-IN-PUBLICATION DATA

Keeney, Bradford P.
    Shamanic Christianity : the direct experience of mystical communion /
Bradford Keeney.
        p. cm.
    Includes bibliographical references and index.
    ISBN 1-59477-086-7 (pbk.)
    1. Christianity and other religions—Shamanism.  2. Shamanism—
Relations—Christianity.  3. Mysticism.     I. Title.
    BR127.K44 2006
    248—dc22

                                                        2005037734

Printed and bound in the United States by Lake Book Manufacturing

10  9  8  7  6  5  4  3  2  1

Text design and layout by Jonathan Desautels
This book was typeset in Sabon with Democratica and Avenir as display
typefaces

To send correspondence to the author of this book, mail a first-class letter
to the author c/o Inner Traditions • Bear & Company, One Park Street,
Rochester, VT 05767, and we will forward the communication.

*Dedicated to my grandparents,*
*Rev. W. L. Keeney and Virginia Keeney*

# CONTENTS

## PART II: THE LOST DIRECTIVES

# PREFACE

I grew up with a grandfather and father who were country preachers, playing the piano in their revival services. Much of my life's work has been devoted to learning from spiritual elders throughout the African diaspora—from South Africa, Namibia, Botswana, Brazil, the Caribbean, and the African American church—whose mystical, shamanic practice of Christianity struck me as the most joyous and liberated form of worship. As this book goes to press, I am in the mountains of the Caribbean island of St. Vincent studying a blend of African spirituality and Christianity known as "shakerism." It emphasizes ecstatic spiritual expression as well as ceremonies devoted to fasting for visionary experiences and shamanic learning. Here I learned some of the great mysteries of being a Christian shaman. Now I am deeply honored to be regarded by my teachers here as a "captain" of the spiritual ships that move through the spirit lands.

The stories and directives that are included in this book were written while I was in an altered state of consciousness inspired by the ecstatic practice of shamanic Christianity. Writing non-stop for several days in a shamanic literary experiment, I wrote the book largely as a continuous stream of prose. The first part of the book, "The Lost Teachings," aims to bring forth the ancestral voices of Christianity. Years ago one of the great spiritual healers of our time, Mama Mona from Soweto, South Africa, performed a ceremony announcing the installation of her spirit guides into me. Her primary guide, Sister Elize, subsequently became my guiding source of inspiration for the lost teachings of shamanic Christianity.

The second part of the book, "The Lost Directives," addresses the least practiced and least understood aspect of many shamanic and spiritual traditions. Here I present the "trickster" side of being a Christian shaman. In alignment with cultural theologian Harvey Cox's classic work *Feast of Fools,* the role of "fool for Christ" is here recast in terms of eccentric action and participation with unorthodox wisdom in everyday life. Whereas the lost teachings are inseparable from altered states, the lost directives encourage "altered traits of living," to borrow Huston Smith's expression.

Many teachers have inspired my work, and I have honored them in previous books I have written and edited. But here I must mention George Hay, my dear friend from New Orleans. A former pastor who became a counselor and college professor, his life is a testimony to the power of deep faith and prayer. Our ongoing conversations have imbued this work.

Finally, I wish to acknowledge my spiritual father, Archbishop Cosmore Pompey of the St. Vincent Shakers. He is a pure Christian shaman and mystic, whose spiritual life has been as amazing as that of anyone I have ever known or read about. His influence on my development as a Christian shaman has been monumental. Love and prayers to his spiritual family in the Caribbean and to all my shamanic sisters and brothers!

# INTRODUCTION
## The Calling Forth of Christian Shamanism

*And it shall come to pass afterward, that I will pour out my spirit on all flesh; your sons and your daughters shall prophesy, your old men shall dream dreams, and your young men shall see visions. Even upon the menservants and maidservants in those days, I will pour out my spirit.*

JOEL 2:28–29

All spiritual traditions, including Christianity, have shamanic roots. When the roots are fed, they sink deeper into the sacred ground. The practices and stories in this book are a calling forth to those who believe they are connected to the teachings and spiritual presence of Jesus. You are invited to feed and water the roots of your spirituality. In this nurturing of your soul, shamanic experience will blossom. This is the way it has always been and shall always be.

Being a Christian shaman involves a radically different way of participating in everyday life. It means that you will sacrifice rarely questioned cultural habits and understandings in favor of honoring innumerable unspoken mysteries. Through the stories and practices of this book you will find a way to undo normality and replace it with the uncommon presence of mystical realization and playful engagement, the two sides of Christian shamanism.

Christian shamans dream sacred visions and feel the ecstatic currents of spirit flowing through their bodies. They get there like the mystics of old—through loving God and praying without end. Mystics and shamans are the same in their devotion to God and in their encounters with the sacred gifts of the Holy Spirit. Christian shamans go further and encourage themselves to reenter the everyday with a transformed posture, that of the Christian trickster, the spiritual contrary who knows that the deepest visions are facilitated by the merriest practices of play.

By following the shamanic exercises spelled out here, you will be able to face the modern dilemmas of our time with a childlike sense of play and wonder. Though you may first feel self-conscious, apprehensive, confused, or baffled by the suggestions that are made, please be mindful that you are being asked to step outside the boundaries that presently define your habitual ways of behaving and constitute what others regard as "consensual reality." Shamanic Christianity asks you to go beyond those constraints and assumptions, making it possible for you to enter a new kingdom of experience. Here the challenges and suffering of life become transformed into lessons of daily enchantment, transcendent ascension, and sacred comedy.

The first part of this book, The Lost Teachings, aims to help you enter into the high mysteries and visions of shamanic Christianity. Through its lessons, you will be well prepared to bring forth sacred dreams and join the grand mystical traditions. The second part of the book, The Lost Directives, introduces exercises involving contrary, or "trickster," actions that help bring you into the uncommon practices of shamanic conduct. Here you find a new way of being in the world and a way of escaping the overseriousness associated with conventional ways of living. The Christian shaman enters the everyday with the spirit of radical experimentalism. No challenge or difficulty is big enough to not be teased inside and out. In the shamanic world, everything is turned around, reversed, deliberately misperceived, tinkered with, and thrown to the elves of merry play.

*Shamanic Christianity* provides a beacon of affirmation for contemporary pilgrims seeking direct communion with spirit. The light begins with one of the greatest shamans in human history, Jesus of Nazareth. But within the temple of Christian light reside other living presences of spiritual guidance. The meditations and stories presented in Part I will reintroduce you to Mary and the historically renowned saints, making them living spiritual teachers for your shamanic life. They will inspire you to seek vision, pray wildly, talk to the animals, receive the holy fire, recognize the sacred light, honor soul-making music, and resurrect your vital participation in life.

The exercises presented in Part II are meant to rekindle the trickster shamanic practices of Christianity that will help you step outside the limitations imposed by cultural expectations and norms for habituated conduct. As your imagination is ignited by the meditations and stories, your behavior will be liberated to enter into the world in an unexpected and spirited way. I invite you to begin the pilgrimage of becoming a Christian shaman. It is a journey that will stretch you in diverse ways. Vertically it will carry you higher into the heavens of visionary inspiration while rooting you more deeply in the daily workings of life on Earth. Horizontally you will be stretched between the sufferings of life simultaneously juxtaposed with absurd play. As you will see, the serious teachings of shamanism must always be countered with the most outrageous forms of nonsense and absurdity. True Christian shamans value the ridiculous as much as they aspire to enter the mystical visions of heaven. No quaking laughter, no entry into the biggest mysteries.

At this very moment stop and ask whether you are feeling too serious about Christian shamanism. Are you smiling or laughing? If neither, you have become too serious. I encourage you to open the book to another page and tickle one word, as if you were tickling a child. Imagine hearing the book giggle. As you enter the shamanic realms, never stop reminding yourself of the importance of hearing that giggle. It must be present in order for the arms of the Christian shaman's cross to stretch. What does that mean? Don't try to figure it out at this time. Instead, set down the book and stretch out your arms. Say to yourself, "I have taken a first step toward finding the lost wisdom of the four-cornered cross."

Forget the feathers, bones, rattles, beads, and the other ceremonial garb that makes up some people's fantasy of what being a shaman is all about. Most of the truly powerful shamans I have met dress normally and carry no magic objects. These authentic shamans often wonder whether the public display of all that paraphernalia is hiding the fact that the displayer has little connection to spirit. The real test of a shaman concerns what you do with your daily habits and the habits of others. This book will teach you how to deal with the issues of daily life, whether it involves your relationships, worries, diet, dealing with boredom, or overcoming bad habits. But it will do so in an unexpected fashion. You will be asked to *play* with the most troubling parts of your life. Warning: this trickster way of tinkering with your life will be unsettling and upsetting to many psychotherapists, ministers, and trained professional people helpers. Don't worry: That's a good sign that shows that you are practicing authentic shamanism.

Here you will be asked to become a child all over again. In the Christian shaman's world you must recover repressed childhood memories, but in this case, I am referring to the forgotten experiences of play and delight that characterize the best moments of childhood. There is simply no way to enter the mystical kingdom without bringing back and utilizing the magical resources of a child's way of being.

Bless those who surrender to sincerely seeking the center of heart with hands of imagination. For these shall make the playful children who will set us free. Christian shamans play in order to release the creative forces within. They stop the habits of overly serious mind so that their inner light may shine. Consider making a vow to bring more frivolity and nonsensical play into your life. Imagine if 50% of your daily experience was absurd and playful. This is your goal: You need half of your life to hold the holy play while the other half is reaching for the serious visions. This is one of the secrets to entering the shamanic mysteries of Christ's children.

We get to the furthest reaches of God's mind through creative imagination, which allows us to leave the grip of the rational, controlling, psychological mind. Any effort to extinguish creative imagination leaves one without any meaningful truth. This is the fallacy of literalism. Those who read the Bible without imagination are killing its deepest and highest truths. Only the act of creative imagination can take us to the most sought-after spiritual depths and heights. This is how we stretch the vertical pole of the cross. While imagination pulls us vertically, absurdity pulls us horizontally. Together these stretchings comprise the Christian shaman's four-cornered cross. You will learn how to stretch your spirit with these poles, the arms and legs of the Christian shaman. Stand up this very moment and lift yourself on your toes while stretching your arms. You have taken another step toward finding the wisdom from the four-cornered cross

You may ask whether the stories and tasks presented here are simply fictions, without credibility because they arose from creative imagination. In answer to this question, I point out that the deeper the imagination and the deeper the unconscious, the further away from conscious deliberation we are taken. Only the conscious mind can lie. The deepest unconscious processes of mind are incapable of lying. They can speak only the truth. As the unconscious escapes the reach of purposeful, conscious, ego mind, it dissolves into a greater collective unconscious, the mind of a greater whole. Some have called this the mind of nature. It is indistinguishable from the mind of God. Here is where the eternal verities are voiced.

Remind yourself that the deeper the truth, the more important that the voice of the sacred giggle be present. Become a fool for Christ. Never forget that without the presence of holy tickling, the doors to perception won't remain open. Tickle yourself again and again. When it is said that the saints could fly or levitate, appreciate the connection between the words "levitate" and "levity." When it is said that the saints saw the sacred light, appreciate that the word to describe what they saw was "light" and not "heavy."

I invite you to challenge the reality you think you know. Seek the visions and the giggling that transform every moment, breath, and heartbeat. Commit yourself to a practice that is deeper because it is lighter. Play with the everyday hells so as to stretch yourself into heaven. Appreciate the ridiculousness associated with becoming a Christian shaman. Stop being so serious about God. Laugh your prayer in order to find the deeper mysteries of God's humor. Cry over the beauty of joy and weep when you are blessed. Become a contrary, a Jesus coyote, a trickster saint, an outstretched cross that juxtaposes endless sacred contraries. As my grandfather, an old country preacher, once said, "All aboard, there's a train heading for glory land." Let us pray, doing so with a not-so-innocent smile:

> *Lord, make us instruments of your divine madness. Make us empty so we can know the fullness of your mysteries. Help us experience who we are not so we can become who we are. Help us be serious about the absurd, and absurd about the serious. Fill our bodies and minds with creative energy and inspired expression. Bring us contrary visions. We rejoice in being spiritual idiots, fools, and imbeciles completely devoted to your unattainable wisdom. For these things we pray. Amen.*

---

Part I
# THE LOST
# TEACHINGS

---

# INTRODUCTION TO THE
# LOST TEACHINGS
*The Mystical Devotions and Practices*

Among Christians there is an almost complete silence about the place of shamanism in experiencing the divine. This is even the case for those who whisper an awareness of Christianity's history of mystics and divine illuminants. Yet shamanic experience is the root form of mystical communion. Shamans, let no one forget, are the sacred technicians who directly communicate with the source of spirit.

When the missionaries came to North America to "save" the Native American Indians, they were sometimes perplexed to discover that while they talked about Jesus, some of the Indians claimed to talk directly with him. Unfortunately, shamanic encounters of divine mysteries were too often discounted and the visionary judged to be mad, or worse, inhabited by evil or satanic influences.

Without direct encounters with spiritual realities, a religion trickles into pale morality, sanctification of the status quo, and metaphysical speculation. Dare anyone ask whether Christians have lost their direct link with the heavens? Is it fair to wonder whether plagues of deafness and blindness have afflicted the theologians, clergy, and parishioners? While the shamanic nature of raw spiritual experience may have been forgotten to a great extent, God has never stopped talking with the faithful and pure of heart.

In the tradition of contemplative practice, I will present this reintroduction of shamanism to Christianity in the form of devotions, which you may use to orient your weekly spiritual practice. The devotions are set forth in four forms. Each begins with a specific *contemplation,* a particular theme or contemplative thought. This is followed by a *meditative focus* enabling the practitioner to create a particular visualization for meditative practice. I then offer a *lost parable,* in the form of a story that has arisen from my own visionary experience. Finally, I prescribe an *active mystical practice* to help ground the meditations and contemplative reflections into a ritual or ceremony that calls for one's active participation. These four forms of mystical devotion and practice are designed to introduce you to both an understanding and an experience of the shamanic tradition of Christianity.

The words and practices that follow are only a spiritual rope, a luminous cord intended to help connect the practitioner to the shamanic core of mystical Christianity. To receive the light of this great faith requires hands willing to grab the rope. At times the going may be tough, an uphill battle requiring sweat and dogged determination. Just as often, you will be able to use the rope to effortlessly and playfully swing across and into the depths of sacred healing and transformation.

Consider setting aside all you have been taught about the characters who first played the original Christian drama. Contemplate the possibility of being introduced to these original ones as holy presences of divine illumination. As living manifestations of the Holy Spirit, they are immediately present to everyone who asks and reaches inwards and outwards with sincerity, humility, and the desire to love all of God's creation.

# 1

# JESUS AS SHAMAN

*Christ was and is the ultimate shaman. . . . In a real sense, every Christian who allows the Spirit to move in him or her is a shaman. . . . An important study might be made comparing the ministry of Jesus with that of shamanism.*

DR. MORTON KELSEY, EPISCOPAL PRIEST,
COUNSELOR, AND AUTHOR

## CONTEMPLATION

We need only mention the story of a man going into the wilderness and surviving spiritual ordeals and temptations to recognize a classic case of shamanic initiation. Shamans throughout history typically have been required to seek solitude in a place of wilderness. While fasting and praying in a place of natural isolation, they confront good and bad spirits and experience a death and rebirth into shamanic reality. They learn to traverse the boundaries separating human beings from alternative ways of being. Thus they receive the mysteries of communing and allying themselves with sacred presences, ancestral spirits, and holy manifestations.

Jesus was no exception to this tradition of initiation in the wilderness. After surviving his ordeals in the desert with the devil, he lived the life of a shaman, performing many extraordinary deeds—from feeding a multitude of people with a few loaves of bread to turning water into wine. Although his shamanic abilities were unparalleled, most of his miracles were performed quietly and without boastful fanfare. It is important to acknowledge that during the time of Jesus, there were many reports of miracles performed by many different shamanic practitioners. These other miracle workers believed they possessed great and privileged power and kept their practices secret and inaccessible.

One of the most remarkable things about Jesus was that he allowed miracles to be seen and understood. He revealed that the source of these miraculous events was not a magic wand, but simple faith that grows into a dynamic presence. As the Bible teaches us, this faith is like a mustard seed, which is the smallest of seeds. But when planted it becomes the largest of the garden plants—it grows into a tree. Perhaps the greatest achievement of Jesus was that he relied not upon the tricks and strategies of shamanic one-upmanship, but instead upon the sacred strength of faith in the divine. His shamanic alchemy was based on the sincere practice of humility, forgiveness, and loving service to others.

While addressing an audience, the disciple Peter summarized the lifetime of Jesus with five short words: "He went about doing good." His life made people "re-contemplate" the nature of God. As philosophers like Huston Smith put it, if God were pure goodness and were to take human form, this incarnation of God would act exactly like Jesus.

The main lesson given by Jesus for shamanic practice concerns the power of goodness. It is the strongest and most effective incantation, magic, and medicine on Earth. The shamanic way of Jesus cultivated a singular focus on the practice of good. He came to Earth and walked among its creatures as the *good shaman*.

## MEDITATIVE FOCUS

Visualize yourself in a vast desert with Jesus at your side. Imagine every great shaman in the history of the world coming up to you and demonstrating his or her magic. One by one you see them each perform powerful and extraordinary acts of alchemy. Merlin creates a forest with a beautiful stream, inviting you to relinquish your dry thirst. Swamis demonstrate their ability to levitate and fly to infinite heavens of pleasure, while Siberian shamans take you on journeys into the mystical underworlds. In the inner landscape of your mind, see the greatest display of shamanic power ever performed.

At the end of this shamanic Olympics, hear Jesus say these words to you:

> *You have seen the great powers that are possible to harness. I offer you a power that is greater than the combination of all these other powers. To receive this power requires that you completely abandon all thirst for any power. When you have become empty of all desire for power, you will understand that the greatest power comes from simply trying to be good. You must be good to all the creatures in the house of my Mother and Father.*

This is the first lesson of the most powerful shaman. Be without power and relinquish the desire for power in order to have all powers at one's disposal.

## LOST PARABLE: JESUS MEETS THE INDIANS

If one believes all the stories about Jesus that have circulated through many different cultures, then Jesus must have walked around the entire world. Among North and South American Indians he was greeted as Kate-Zahl and Mahnt-Azoma, among other names. Other legends say that after visiting the South Pacific, he arrived on the west coast of South America near Peru and visited many Indian tribes. The Ojibway Indians who lived on the shores of Mishegahme in Michigan were among the ones who knew of the man with a beard who performed many healings. He eventually went up to Canada accompanied by a couple of wolves. Because of their reverence for animals, the Indian people respected him and followed his advice.

In the story that follows I will tell what I believe Jesus taught other shamans as he walked around the world. We do know one fact that not a single custodian of the oldest cultural stories would argue with. It is agreed that wherever Jesus went, he was immediately acknowledged as the kindest shaman anyone had ever met.

Our story begins in Canada, at a time when Jesus had arrived at a small encampment of Ojibway Indians near what is now known as Lac La Croix. The Indian elders had already dreamed of his arrival. In their dreams, they had seen how he had walked on water and had raised the dead. They respected his great shamanic gifts before he had even stepped on their soil.

They greeted Jesus with a sacred ceremony and taught him that the pipe was a spiritual umbilical cord connecting their hearts and minds to Mother Earth and the Great Spirit. Jesus wept with joy over the sincere and wise humility of these Indian people. They shared many stories and before he left, he warned them about a time when black robes would arrive on their shore and pretend to be his friends. Jesus told the Indians, "No matter what the black robes say or do, they are to be understood as having been sent by the Great Spirit to learn from the Indian elders."

"What will make the black robes' learning difficult," Jesus forewarned, "is their mental condition." He explained that each of these black robes would suffer from the spiritual disease of arrogance. "They will think they know all there is to know. Their disease will have progressed to the point that they will forget they need to learn from the Indians."

Jesus advised the Ojibway elders to tell these black robes that some of the Indian holy people speak directly to the Messiah. "When the robed ones arrive," Jesus directed, "tell them the stories of my life in Galilee. They will be shocked to find that you know these things." He went on to say:

*When they ask how you know me, tell them you know how to speak to me. Most of them won't believe you and will be frightened by the possibility that I am still alive. But a few, a very small number, will come to you and ask how they may meet you. You are then to remind them of how all shamans must go into the wilderness to find their spiritual voice, eyes, and ears. It is there that they learn to see, hear, speak, and act in the world of spirit. If they continue to be sincere and humble, take them into the woods as you have for others over the centuries. If they are impeccable in facing their raw, naked mind, then I will introduce myself to them.*

*I will tell them to ask you about the holy nature of the pipe and ask them to honor its practice. You will then receive them with the respect due any human being who has opened the shamanic door to the other worlds.*

The Ojibway elders understood what Jesus had told them. They gave him a pipe and held a great feast to celebrate the importance of their time together. Jesus gave them the tiny cross he carried around his neck and said, "These four directions make us the same."

He went off with the wolves by his side and traveled all the way to what is now Nova Scotia. There he was received by the Micmac Indians, to whom he gave the same instructions.

After Jesus left the North American native peoples, the wolves deeply missed him. No human being had ever been as understanding and as caring to them as Jesus. Not a single wolf ever forgot his tender touch. From that day on, the wolves sang at the moon in the same way they had sung with Jesus. He asked them to never stop singing this way, so that their hearts would always be able to reach him across the evening sky. There is not one wolf today that doesn't know the shamanic song of Jesus. They are the ones who taught Jesus to sing, and they keep the heart of Jesus present on our fragile planet.

## ACTIVE MYSTICAL PRACTICE

Take a walk into the woods, carrying a tiny cross with you. Find a special spot that seems peaceful to you and sit there. Meditate on the relationship Jesus had with the wolves. Imagine them singing together. Wait until dark, knowing that you will sing like a wolf this evening. When the time feels right, hold your cross tightly and howl with as much sincerity and strength as you can muster. Imagine the heart of Jesus awakening the light of his goodness within your own heart.

Take the cross home and place it over a photograph of a wolf howling. Keep this image of the connection between Jesus and the wolves in a place you regard as private and holy.

# 2

# MARY AND THE RELIGION OF THE GREAT MOTHER

*Christianity was born and preached first in cultures in
which feasts and celebrations were an organic and essential part of the whole world-view and way of life. . . . And,
whether we like it or not, Christianity accepted and
made its own this fundamentally human phenomenon
of feast, as it accepted and made its own the whole
man and all his needs.*

ALEXANDER SCHEMANN,
*SACRAMENTS AND ORTHODOXY*

## CONTEMPLATION

The fact that Mary is mentioned in only about a dozen passages in the
New Testament has done nothing to dampen the effects of her divine
inspiration as a spiritual mother throughout the world. As early as the
second century AD, scholars advanced the idea that the Virgin Mary is
none other than the Great Mother or Mother Goddess. This feminine
embodiment of the Holy Spirit has been known under many names,
including Mother of the Gods by the Phrygians, Minerva by the Athe-
nians, Venus by the Cyrenaicans, Diana by the Cyrians and Cretans,

Prosperine by the Sicilians, Ceres by the Eleusinians, Isis by the Egyptians, Demeter by the Greeks, and Kali by the Hindus.

The Religion of the Great Mother is known by the South African Zulu as a religion emphasizing relationship, ecology, stewardship, and caring. It is distinct from the Religion of the Father, which is more the stuff of lone cowboy heroes seeking fame and fortune regardless of the impact on and cost to others. Too often, the latter has characterized the mainstream Christian Church and its mark on the natural world. However, even in the early days of Christianity, there were people who practiced the Religion of the Great Mother by venerating Mary. They created a Marian Church that existed side by side with the official church.

One group, the Collyridians, was made up chiefly of women and women priests. Their main ritual involved the offering of small cakes (in Greek, *collyris* means "small cake"). These cake-serving worshippers of the Great Mother claimed that the Virgin Mary went off into a wilderness area and founded their community after being rejected by the early leaders of the church. The Collyridians and other Marian Churches were subsequently condemned as heretics by the male-dominated traditional church.

The great miracle is that in spite of the many historical attempts to silence what could be known about Mary, whether in the New Testament or in the churches she founded, she is still very much alive for Christian practitioners. In contemporary times, more apparitions of Mary are seen than of Jesus Christ. Devotees of Mary undertake pilgrimages to the shrines associated with these apparitions. Each year, one and a half million people visit 140 Rue du Bac in Paris, four and a half million visit Lourdes, and twelve million visit the basilica of Our Lady of Guadalupe in Mexico. For a silent voice so often kept hidden, Mary's image has broken through all the silencing and ignited the souls of millions.

## MEDITATIVE FOCUS

Imagine being in an ancient kitchen with the Virgin Mother Mary. The two of you are baking some loaves of bread and Mary says:

*We'll put some special yeast in these loaves that will surprise even Jesus. When he tries to feed a multitude, he will be amazed to find that these few loaves can handle the job.*

In this guided meditation, listen to your conversation with Mary and how she explains why she never told Jesus that it was she who anointed the bread in this special way. Hear Mary respond with these words:

*Jesus must learn that he knows nothing about feeding the hungry if he knows nothing about making a loaf of bread. The real magic in our world, greater than all the tricks of shamans, takes place in the kitchen, particularly in the oven. Too many men have not learned this alchemy of transformation. Knowing how to make bread is the first step toward understanding the miracle of birth and all the other mysteries of life and death. We women have always known this, even when we have denied that we know it. Someday men, including Jesus, will learn the Religion of the Great Mother and revere the way bread is made before it is served to others.*

## LOST PARABLE: MARY SPEAKS
## THE MYSTICAL, ETERNAL SILENCE

All biblical scholars are aware of how little is written about Mary and how few words she speaks in the Bible. What they do not always learn, however, is that her silence may be the most outspoken wisdom in all of Christendom. Followers of the gnostic teacher and poet Valentinus prayed to Mary as the "mystical, eternal silence." They knew that the greatest wisdom of all was that which could not be spoken. The mother who gave birth to Jesus was the holder of divine wisdom, and her silence became the light of wisdom sought by millions of pilgrims.

Mary, like other shamans, went into the wilderness to be initiated into the realms of sacred knowledge. God spoke to her, telling her she would be shown the wisdom of the spiritual universe. It began when a small, four-legged desert creature came to Mary and said:

*Our Creator has spoken and asked me to open the door to your anointing. I must warn you that no one has ever been shown all of God's wisdom. To receive this infinite awareness is to become the Mother of God. You will no longer need to speak, because you will know that what is known can only be birthed and created, not spoken. You will see that you must create and make life with all the other gods and goddesses. Your first birth will be the son of light, Jesus. After that, God will allow you to make anything you choose.*

Mary thought long and hard about what God's little creature had told her. She finally said, "I am ready to die and be reborn so I can give birth to what God already knows." The little creature quietly responded, "And what do you want to spend your life creating? Do you want to sculpt, create new worlds, invent entire kingdoms, paint, or compose majestic symphonies?"

Mary knew exactly what she wanted to create. Without any hesitation she responded, "I want to make the most perfect little cakes that will bring joy to all who receive them. With one small bite people will know that heavenly happiness is attainable and is worth attaining."

"So be it!" bellowed the voice of an elder woman, who seemed to speak from a cloud that had rolled onto the desert.

Mary returned to give birth to the Son of Light. She then went back to the desert. She and other women proceeded to make the most delicious small cakes anyone has ever tasted. Anyone fortunate enough to taste one of these masterpieces would be unable to keep from saying out loud, "Why, I think I've died and gone to heaven!"

The shamanic mystery of Mary's life centers around the way she and her followers saw that every human being would be able to receive at least several of these miraculous tastings in a lifetime. We each are able to receive a taste of heaven's existence, through a small cake, a loaf of bread, or some food made for us by our own mother or by someone else acting under the influence of the Holy Mother.

Followers of the Great Holy Mother know that treasures created for others are the most powerful teachings of the holy light. Mothers and practitioners of mothering make cakes or poems or stories or songs or acts of good deeds as a form of celebrating and participating with the Supreme God in creating a living heaven on Mother Earth herself.

## ACTIVE MYSTICAL PRACTICE

Learn to bake a wonderful small cake. If you don't know how to cook, then learn. If you already cook, then set your mind on learning how to do it more thoughtfully and masterfully.

Find and try many recipes for small cakes, and have your friends and family tell you which cake is "the most heavenly." When you find this sacred recipe, whether it takes you weeks, months, or years, proceed to fill the world with as many of these little cakes as you can. Give them to colleagues, friends, neighbors, and family. Become known as "the baker of those heavenly cakes."

Don't forget to tell people that you call your masterpiece "heavenly cakes." If they ask why you make and give away so many cakes, tell them the story of the Collyridians. Explain that this is your way of worshipping the Great Mother.

# 3

# ST. FRANCIS AND
# THE TEACHINGS OF
# THE FOREST

*Thou shalt not be on friendly terms*
*With guys in advertising firms,*
*Nor speak with such*
*As read the Bible for its prose,*
*Nor, above all, make love to those*
*Who wash too much.*

W. H. AUDEN, "UNDER WHICH LYRE?
A REACTIONARY TRACT FOR THE TIMES"

## CONTEMPLATION

Francis of Assisi, one of the most loved saints of all time, entered the world of mystery when he heard a voice coming from a crucifix in the small, almost ruined church of San Damiano of Assisi: "Go and repair my house, which is falling down." He obeyed this voice and, after arguing with his wealthy father, renounced his inheritance, removed his clothes, and walked off into the woods to be with the earthly creatures of God's creation.

Eventually, he and his disciples begged for money and rebuilt San Damiano by their own labor. Inside this church Francis read the gospel with such devotion that men were unable to hold back their tears. Declaring himself wed to Lady Poverty, Francis devoted his life to the quest for the crucified Christ. In 1224 he experienced the impression of the stigmata on Mount La Verna, receiving the scars of Christ while in a mystical state of ecstasy. On that day, his flesh became identical to the Savior's, a reflection of his lifetime commitment to identifying with the suffering of Christ.

Francis was best known for his close relationship with the animal kingdom. One of the most famous scenes of his life was his preaching to the birds. His friendship with the wolf of Gubbio became very well known, and this wolf was buried in the local church. St. Francis's most important teaching was how important it is that we learn to identify with all the created beings and manifestations of the universe. As his life beautifully exemplified, becoming one with God's creation moves one closer to the hands of the Creator.

## MEDITATIVE FOCUS

Take an imaginary walk into the most enchanted forest you can visualize. In the middle of this sacred place is an absolutely serene blue lake with an island in its center. A canoe awaits you and carries you to the island. Gathered on the island are all the living creatures of the forest. They have come together to meet you.

As you begin to realize the miracle of this moment, a white cloud drops from the sky and transforms itself into the shape of St. Francis. He speaks directly to you with a gentle, caring voice:

*God's creatures have come here today so your heart will be opened to seeing me. They have taught you that miracles are possible and this learning enables us to meet. Know that these creatures are the most holy teachers. They will teach you how to be a member of the great community of all living beings. Close your eyes so your heart will be able to see them more vividly and your ears will be able to hear them more clearly. Be still and wait for their teachings to drift into your deepest imagination.*

In your private stillness, wait for a creature to speak or show you something. Perhaps the message will not be accessible to your vision and hearing, but instead will evoke feelings that bring deeper appreciation. With time, the creatures may take you into the center of the lake and introduce you to the teachers who live in the water. A whole lifetime of learning awaits those who learn how to be still and accept our equality and relationship with other living teachers. These great mystery teachings of St. Francis instruct us to live as simply and freely as the birds in the sky.

## LOST PARABLE: ST. FRANCIS AND THE WOLF OF GUBBIO

From time to time Francis would venture into the forest to speak to the animals. His followers never knew exactly what he did, but they all were aware of his special relationship with the creatures of the woods. It took many centuries to find out what actually transpired with St. Francis and God's creatures, particularly the wolf of Gubbio.

It began one cold autumn morning. Francis had been unable to sleep the night before. Every time he closed his eyes, he would see a forest with a beautiful lake. On an island in the middle of this body of water lived a wolf that Francis believed was calling him. After seeing this wolf in his imagination throughout the entire night, Francis decided to take off on a journey to see if he could find the source of this mystery.

Francis went into a forest, believing that it might have a lake similar to the one he had seen in his fantasies. When he came to such a body of water, he was surprised to find that it had an island in its center. To the best of his memory he had never seen the island before. With haste Francis removed his clothes and swam toward the land. He arrived shivering with cold as the sky began to darken. As the wilderness lost its daylight, he noticed a glowing flicker of light amid the trees. He walked toward it and discovered a fire made of dried timber. Francis fell to his knees and thanked the Creator for providing him with the gift of natural warmth.

He soon fell asleep and had a dream. In the forest of his dreams,

Francis met the wolf that had been calling out for him. This wolf spoke to him and told him a story he would never forget:

> Many years ago, I became loyal to the same master you have given your life to following. He traveled all over the world and I was fortunate to accompany him on his trips to faraway places. This man was a great shaman from Nazareth whose mother had asked the wolves to walk with him and teach him to sing.
>
> We gladly walked with Jesus on his many journeys, and we became the best of friends. If you want to follow in his steps, you, too, must learn to be one with us. We will protect you and teach you how to sing. It is the singing that will connect you to the heart of your Divine Savior. Tonight I will teach you to sing in your dreams. Come, we must go to a sacred place and sing together.

Francis woke up, and sitting right before him was the wolf he had seen in his dreams. He followed the wolf to a bluff overlooking a deep meadow. Together they sang at the moon and Francis began to feel as if he were a wolf dreaming of being a man. As far as he knew, he sang all through the night. As the wolf had promised, the singing brought him next to his master. In his heart he could see the cross of Jesus.

Francis returned to his community and never told a single person about what had taken place in the forest. A year went by, and it was autumn again. To his surprise he began feeling the call of the wolf and the forest again. Being a most obedient servant of the faith, he immediately took off on another journey to find the wolf.

Again the warm fire awaited Francis, and in his dreams the wolf came to him and spoke:

> It is time for me to return and walk with you. When you awaken I will be with you and will become a part of your life. But before we return to your place in the world, there is something I must show you.

At that moment the wolf looked up at the sky. Francis followed its action and also looked up. In the evening sky a great movement of the stars had taken place and created the image of Christ hanging on the cross. Hundreds, perhaps thousands of wolves began howling their sacred song. To Francis's great amazement, the moon became brighter and brighter until he could see moonbeams going directly to each of the four corners of the cross on which Jesus hung. As the moonbeams bathed the cross, Jesus began turning into pure light. When he was completely transformed into light, he was freed from the cross and flew to the moon, encircling it as a halo.

The wolf turned to Francis and said, "Now you have seen the unspoken mystery that binds the wolves and Jesus together in their sacred song toward the moon." Francis was so overwhelmed with the ecstasy of this vision that he could not think or speak. He was able only to weep.

He returned to a small town named Gubbio as the wolf walked by his side. On every full moon thereafter, Francis and the wolf of Gubbio would go off into the woods and howl at the moon. In this way Francis learned to become one with the crucified Christ and earned his halo of holy light.

## ACTIVE MYSTICAL PRACTICE

Go to a religious bookstore or gift shop and purchase a small picture of St. Francis. On a separate piece of paper, draw a picture of the moon that is at least the same size as the picture of St. Francis. On the inside of this moon draw the figure of Christ's cross. Draw light beams showering out of this cross in all directions.

Glue the back side of your picture of St. Francis onto this moon, making certain that the heart of St. Francis is aligned over the center of the cross. Obtain a *Farmer's Almanac* and mark all the days having a full moon for the entire year. Keep these dates in your personal calendar. On the evening of a full moon, place this specially prepared picture of St. Francis under your pillow and visualize being with him in the forest where he learned from the animals, particularly his faithful friend, the wolf of Gubbio.

# 4

# HILDEGARD AND THE FIRE OF MYSTICAL ILLUMINATION

*And it came to pass . . . when I was 42 years and 7 months old, that the heavens were opened and a blinding light of exceptional brilliance flowed through my entire brain. And so it kindled my whole heart and breast like a flame, not burning but warming. . . .*
HILDEGARD OF BINGEN

## CONTEMPLATION

Hildegard of Bingen was a Benedictine nun and mystical visionary who was encouraged to write down her visions in a work entitled *Scivias* (referring to "one who knows the ways of the Lord"). These visions inspired her to create poems, plays, works of science and medicine, illustrations, and music.

Hildegard believed a "man in sapphire blue" resides in every human being and constitutes a divine presence. One of our shamanic possibilities is to reawaken this inner spirit. One of the ways to make our way to the blue man is through music. In Hildegard's compositions, collectively entitled *Symphony of the Harmony of Heavenly Revelations*, she gives musical form to her mystical encounters with the light of Christ.

She believed that when sung, this music could deliver mystical vibrations directly to the soul and help awaken our mystical sensitivities. Her sacred music aimed to transmit the vibrations of Christ's holy light and awaken our inner blue man.

One of the most important teachings of Hildegard was her belief that the light of God shines through us in all our acts of creativity. Like other mystics and shamans, she believed humans must be awakened by divine light in order to become the vehicles through which the gods create their great works. Mystical and shamanic experiences thus help prepare us to co-create with the Great Spirit. When the holy light shines through us, it can manifest its creative transformations, modulations, and expressions in infinite possible ways.

Hildegard reminds us that creative expression is the most powerful way to practice spirituality, more powerful than giving "right answers" or mindless and irresponsible obedience to officials of social hierarchies. In her own words, "There is wisdom in all creative works." The expression of creativity carries the heart of truth in itself and has little to do with any subsequent evaluation or interpretation.

In her own communing and co-creating with the divine, Hildegard recognized the Holy Mother as a goddess and understood the relational basis of the Religion of the Great Mother, that the core of mystical understanding and illumination concerns the interrelatedness of all things. Hildegard expressed this primary insight in the twelfth century:

Everything that is in the heavens, on the earth, and under the earth,
is penetrated with connectedness, penetrated with relatedness. . . .
God has arranged everything in the universe in consideration of
everything else.

## MEDITATIVE FOCUS

Imagine a blue light inside your solar plexus that only has been turned on a couple of times in your entire life. Allow this light to come on again now and imagine its energy is making your belly warm or hot. When the light feels "blue hot," transform it into the shape of a blue man who is ancient, wise, and loving.

Picture this inner blue man slowly climbing up your spinal column and entering your heart. Inside your heart the blue man is transformed into pure white light. Allow this light to form the image of Jesus, the source of absolute divine light.

See the light of Jesus shooting out of his fingertips, then coming into and moving through each of your fingers, ears, eyes, and mouth. Stare at this image of your illumination.

See yourself, in your mind's eye, beginning some kind of creative work—writing, sewing, painting, or whatever else you might choose. Make certain that the light is shooting out of you so that it shapes and guides the movement of your creativity. Experience how ecstatic the act of creation can be when you perform it while in a state of illumination.

## LOST PARABLE: HILDEGARD AND THE VIBRATION OF THE SOUL

As a mystic familiar with shamanic experiences, Hildegard once woke up in the middle of the night to the sound of a single vibrating note. She did not know the source of this vibration, but assumed it was some invisible singer. When she stopped the sleuthing activity of her rational mind and fully attended to the sound, her whole body began moving in sync with the sound's vibrations.

As her body rocked back and forth with the movement of the sound, she began having visions of mystical illumination. An inner voice told her to close her eyes so she could see with newly washed eyes. Doing this, she found sight with her eyes closed. What she saw did not look like the typical outer world, but was every bit as real as what others see with their eyes open.

The inner world had depth and texture and color and definition. It was illuminated by an inner eye that could not only see, but could also trace the image of any inner vision. She was shown how to move her arm so that it was guided by her inner eye. In this way she learned to draw. This drawing was an inner eye tracing an inner image, causing a corresponding movement of a pencil or brush in her hand. She believed the experience to be so unusual that it would be impossible for anyone to understand what she was talking about.

For years she practiced making divine illustrations in this mystical way. Her inner world revealed many designs, images, and forms that she simply traced onto paper, guided by her inner eye.

One day there were no images. All that was presented was a sound. What was strange was that she could somehow feel the shape of the sound and produce an image of it. Over the years she was able to make many sketches of these holy sounds. After she had created an extensive collection of these inner drawings of sight and sound, she had a vision of her inner blue man turning into a blue body of water. The water began to fill her whole inner body. When she was completely filled, she felt she had become the blue man.

At that moment the inner water began to boil. She did not experience any pain, but was aware of an inner transformation. The water boiled, turned to steam, and then broke into a burning flame. The whole of her being became a flame of illumination. It cleansed every thought, feeling, perception, and experience she had ever had in her life. The fire burned her mystical insides into absolute nothingness.

When the fire stopped she looked with her inside eyes and saw the eye of God, who was the source of the flame, the light, and the great nothingness. God spoke:

> You may only look once. I have cleared an unobstructed path so you may see the source of illumination. Once you see the source you will be unable to see anything else in the world except my light. You will then know that your inside has become my outside. This is the gift of illumination. Use it to light the fires of others so the world may learn to see and create once again.

Hildegard spent the rest of her life creating all she could create with the hope that others would experience her work as holding holy vibrations that would help them begin moving. She knew there was no actual knowledge to acquire. For Hildegard, learning was the gift of becoming illuminated so that the holy light could spread its rays into creative works.

During her lifetime, she helped many people to be awakened by these holy rays. When she died, the custodians of darkness did what they could to cover the light of her creative work. Many centuries later, a small four-legged creature was exploring a meadow in Germany and came across an opening in the ground. Inside this cavelike structure were the carefully preserved illustrations of the divine light drawn by Hildegard.

The creature, a fox, immediately was illuminated and anointed. The spirit of Hildegard spoke to the fox and asked if it would walk the Earth reintroducing her illuminations and vibrations to the world. She promised to turn the creature into a human being and give him the biblical name of a saint. The fox, whom Hildegard named Matthew, went forth into the world as a disguised creature of illumination and planted many seeds of light wherever he went.

## ACTIVE MYSTICAL PRACTICE

Sit in a chair and light one candle, placing it in front of you. Light another candle and place it behind you. As you sit and stare at the candle flame in front of you, pretend you are looking at the one behind you. Practice this for many nights and see if you can have the experience of believing you see the candle behind you for at least two seconds. Practice this for at least one month.

When you are almost ready to give up trying, turn around and stare at the candle flame behind you. Realize your mind is more familiar with the former candle, the one that was in front of you. Pretend you are sitting facing forward, but that the candle you now behold is actually the one behind you.

After exercising your inner eye with this exercise, hold an unlit candle in each hand. Keep your eyes closed as you practice seeing them inside your imagination. When you are able to light the image of your inner candles, get rid of the outer candles and practice keeping your inner candle lit. Every evening before retiring, tell yourself that if you learn to light your inner candle, it will only be a matter of time before it sets fire to your inside and cleanses your whole being. With this simple preparation, you may become illuminated by the great divine light and be transformed into a lighthouse for others.

# 5

# TALKING TO ANIMALS AND FAIRIES: THE CELTIC SAINTS

*The belief in fairies is quite a living thing here yet. For example, old Mrs. K., about a year ago, told me that on one occasion, when her daughter had been in Castletown during the day, she went out to the road at nightfall to see if her daughter was yet in sight, whereupon a whole crowd of fairies suddenly surrounded her, and began taking her off toward South Barrule Mountain; and, she added, "I couldn't get away from them until I had called my son."*

REV. J. M. SPICER,
VICAR OF MALEW PARISH,
CASTLETOWN, IRELAND*

## CONTEMPLATION

Between the fifth and twelfth centuries the Celtic Church thrived in northern England, Wales, Scotland, Brittany, and the whole of Ireland. The creative and shamanic practitioners of Celtic spirituality revered

---

*Cited in *The Fairy Faith in Celtic Countries* by W. Y. Evans-Wentz, Citadel Press, 1990.

poetic imagination, heartfelt stories, and visionary dreams. During this time, the Celtic saints carried the holy light while the Dark Ages darkened the spiritual roadways for most Europeans.

The Celtic saints honored their relations with all living things. It was not uncommon for them to speak with animals and have encounters with angels, fairies, and spirit guides. With respect to the wee ones, Carolyn White, an authority on Irish fairies, reports that Father O'Flynn lived with the fairies for one hundred and one years, and when he returned he was regarded as a holy man and instantly made a priest.

The Celtic saints were most at home communing with their animal friends. Saint Kevin of Glendalough went on a spiritual fast when a blackbird flew into his open palm. Kevin did not move his hand, allowing the bird to build her nest in it and remain until her brood had hatched. While he held the nest, an angel appeared and told Kevin he did not need to continue holding it. He replied, "It is no great thing for me to bear this pain of holding my hand under the blackbird for the sake of heaven's king, for upon the cross of suffering Jesus bore every pain on behalf of Adam's seed."

Saint Ciaran was also no stranger to the animal kingdom. He had a fox carry his written letters. One day, while he was studying a book, a stag came up to him and allowed him to place the book on the deer's horns. Stories such as these were not uncommon.

During a time of famine, Ciaran decided to bake some bread, and prayed it would please the elders. An angel came to him, and the bread he baked was the best anyone had ever tasted. He knew the holy recipe for mystical manna, the same bread baked by the children of Israel. Everyone who ate Ciaran's bread was healed from sickness and filled with exuberant joy. It is not known whether Ciaran knew about the Collyridians.

One of my favorite Celtic saints was Maedoc of Ferns. He was born in Ireland in the last part of the sixth century. Ordained as a bishop by the pope in Rome, he founded several Irish monasteries, including one in County Leitrim. His name means "son of the star" and was derived from the story of how he was born. His father, a king named Setna, and his mother, Eithne, fasted and prayed for God to give them a child. One night they each had the same vision of a star falling from the sky and entering Eithne's mouth. It was on that night that Maedoc was conceived.

Bright rays of light remained a long time on the spot where he was born. Maedoc became friends with many animals and particularly enjoyed the companionship of wolves. Years later when he took a pilgrimage to Rome to be ordained bishop, a miracle took place. When he entered the city of Rome, all the bells in the city began ringing on their own, unassisted by any human hands. It is also said that God gave him the sacred gift of a staff left on the altar of Peter. Maedoc later used this holy staff to raise a woman from the dead. There seem to be no end to the stories about his shamanic practices. He once walked across waves of water on the ocean. At another time he was observed climbing a golden ladder reaching from Earth to heaven.

Perhaps the most remarkable story about Maedoc was his encounter with a starving, weak mother wolf. Maedoc came upon the starving wolf on a walk with a young boy. He asked the boy if he had any food to give the wolf and the boy said he only had one loaf of bread and a piece of fish. Maedoc asked for the food and gave it to the wolf. He then asked the boy to bring him some leaves from the forest. The boy did so and Maedoc blessed the leaves, turning them into bread and fish, which he gave to the boy.

On no other place on Earth are there more stories of joy and mystery than on the emerald island of Ireland. The holy radiance of the early Celtic saints still lives today in the truth passed on through these stories. These tales lie asleep in the blood of all Irish folks and can be felt by anyone whose heart beats in time with the shamanic drumming of the little fairies who roam underneath the soil of all souls.

## MEDITATIVE FOCUS

Create the image of lying on a green pasture somewhere in the countryside of Ireland. There you have been reading a book about the Celtic saints and your head is filled with many stories about how they talked with animals, angels, fairies, and other spirits. Imagine falling asleep on the green grass of Ireland and having a dream about one of these saints.

In this dream a saint comes up to you and says, "I have a message from your guardian angel. She says you need to write her a letter." In the dream, you awaken to write a letter to your guardian angel. You tell her about your dream and all the things you've learned about the early shamanic practices of Christianity.

You address your letter as follows:

To:  My Guardian Angel
     Heavenly Sky

See yourself dropping this letter in a mailbox near an old Celtic church. Visualize your guardian angel receiving and reading your letter. See her sitting down at her desk and writing a letter back to you. Look at what she is writing and read the letter you hope she would actually write to you.

## LOST PARABLE: THE CAVE OF DONEGAL

For the Irish and all others with Ireland in their hearts, there is no difference between nature and spirit. As Celtic scholar Christopher Bamford writes, "Christianity and the act of Christ was never an end in itself" but a "divine means" to achieve the holy state "for which all creation was intended, [and which] was always in Ireland." In early times, Irish Christian pilgrims went to sacred underground places to have shamanic death and resurrection experiences. St. Patrick's Purgatory in County Donegal was used for this very purpose. Lying on an island in Red Lake, it is a cave where early Christians entered to seek holy visions. The story that follows is about a pilgrim who went into this holy cave and was never seen coming out.

Long ago a young lady decided to visit the holy cave in Donegal to see if she could have herself a vision. Following all the appropriate preparations, the priests and priestesses approved her undergoing the sacred ritual. In an evening ceremony conducted with many lit candles, she sincerely listened to the people's stories of having their lives completely transformed by their fast in the cave.

The advice she and others received as preparation for the fast in the cave was easy to understand, but difficult for some to faithfully exercise. Each initiate to the cave was required to give up one habit before beginning travel to the sacred site. This young lady, named Katie, gave up eating the little sweet cakes she had grown fond of when she was a little girl.

The other preparation required adopting a new habit in one's life that involved helping others in some way. Katie chose to paint tiny pictures of fairies and give them away to children. With each picture she painted, she committed herself to attaching a story written for the child. She had always dreamed of being a writer and a painter, but was shy about showing her work to any older person. This new habit would enable her to do so without worrying about her art being judged by anyone else.

Katie was given a special prayer service before entering the cave and was shown a hot spring where she bathed and made herself ready. Her guide at the cave told her to focus on what inspired her heart and to sing out loud whenever she believed her mind was beginning to distract her. If she was sincere and persevered, it was possible the Holy Spirit would take pity on her and give her a vision.

Following her guide, Katie descended into the deepest part of the cave, where it was very dark and damp. She could hear every sound of every breath she made. No amount of preparation could have made her ready for the depth of isolation the cave brought about.

She began singing during her first hour in the cave and found it comforting. Losing track of time, she drifted in and out of sleep. After two days she did not know whether she was dreaming of being awake or awake wondering whether she was dreaming. She continued to sing even though her voice had weakened to that of a whisper.

On the third day of isolation Katie thought she saw a flickering light. It became brighter and brighter and was finally revealed as a tiny torch held by a tiny fairy. The fairy introduced herself as Rose O'Sullivan and proceeded to sing the silliest songs Katie had ever heard. Katie forgot about her thirst and hunger and fear and became completely enthralled with the antics and performance of Rose. With her music and wit, Rose charmed Katie into the world of fairies. The more drawn in she became, the more other fairies appeared. First it was Patrick, and then Eire, Finn, and Lady Ruad. All these little people sang silly songs and charmed Katie deeper into the fairy world.

When she was fully inside the fairy underworld, the fairies played their harps for her. Never had she heard such beautiful, melancholy music. It broke her heart and filled her soul at the same time. She saw that the fairies were master poets, storytellers, painters, and musicians. Since Katie had decided to paint and tell stories, they were interested in showing her their world.

Katie lived with the fairies for five hundred years, but did not age a year. She learned how to make herself invisible and to make herself heard through the art of indirection. What this means is she became a master storyteller who could give the appearance of telling a silly, simple story that was actually a very serious message in disguise. All these things she mastered while living with the fairies.

By the time she left the cave no one was visiting it anymore. The Celtic Church had been destroyed by a Christianity that had lost its connection to shamanism. The whole world had changed, and the cave had been completely forgotten.

The last thing the fairies told her before she reentered the outside world was that others like her were also returning from the fairy world. The fairies had spent centuries passing on their wisdom to hundreds of humans who had sought vision in the holy cave. Katie eventually discovered that she and others like her had entered the twenty-first century and were making poems, stories, paintings, and music, among other aesthetic practices.

Katie and her friends discovered certain signs that provided a fairly good indication that a person had fairy knowledge. If you find yourself exhibiting these behaviors, it is likely you are one of these underworld alumni. One sign involves seeking literature others might regard as weird, absurd, esoteric, or ridiculous. Another revealing characteristic is a fascination with the possibility that people were once able to talk with animals, angels, fairies, and spirits. However, the most obvious indication is when a person loves to eat little sweet cakes while laughing about things others would find strange. If this sounds anything like you, chances are you have fairy knowledge, and Katie and her friends will someday find you.

## ACTIVE MYSTICAL PRACTICE

Go to a toy store and purchase some tiny plastic figures of people. Select five of them to be your fairies. Give each a name and make up a story about what they are skilled at performing. Cut a piece of green paper into the shape of Ireland. Place this green island under your bed and set your five named and storied fairies on it.

Before going to sleep each night, peek under your bed and say, "Goodnight, my fairy friends. Maybe tonight you will take me to the fairy underworld. If you happen to see a saint, please pass on my greetings."

Make a commitment to maintain this practice for twelve months. When you dream of the fairy people, write down your dream on green paper cut into the same size and shape as the Ireland shape under your bed. Glue it to the Ireland shape. As your entries into the fairy underworld become more numerous, realize that your island will become thicker and have more depth. Should you ever be taught something by a fairy, ask the little one to introduce you to the Celtic saint of your choice. If you are lucky enough to meet the saint in your dreams, be sure you place a four-leaf clover on the heart of your Ireland.

# 6

# MIRACLE Of
# THE HOLY LIGHT

*While ye have light, believe in the light, that ye may be the children of light.*

JOHN 12:36

## CONTEMPLATION

A most remarkable mystery of the Greek Orthodox Church takes place every year and is called the Eastern Miracle of the Holy Light of Jerusalem. A holy light appears at the Church of the Resurrection that once housed Jesus' cross and tomb. On this holiday, also known as Holy Saturday, the holy light never fails to light up the vigil on the Lord's tomb. The holy light also makes itself manifest to many believers.

Paul Pappas provides a personal testimony from one of the guards of the tomb:*

He heard a soft sound as if caused by the wind, and then saw a blue light that filled the entire chamber but turned for a while like a powerful tornado before becoming motionless. The Patriarch, he

---

*Paul Pappas, *Jesus' Tomb in India*. Asian Humanities Press, 1991, page 149.

said, who was all covered by this Holy Light, began to read the prayer book, aided by an illumination coming from this strange Light, which had begun to turn again and suddenly burst into a brilliant white glow.

According to Tsekoura, the holy light also appears to crowds of people outside the chapel.* It appears "in white and blue colors, moving about rapidly from left to right and up and down . . . [it] may light up the face of one person or of a group of faithful [and] may appear as a radiant cloud, a lighted disk, or a radiant garment, lit up balls, fire or fires, a shiny crown, or a heavenly light." Although it always manifests itself on Holy Saturday, it has been seen on other days as well.

The holy light at the Church of the Resurrection reminds us of how often the Holy Spirit manifests itself as light. This is true for spiritual traditions throughout the world. Let us never forget that Jesus came to the world as a great illuminator and any mystical practice relating to his spirit usually casts rays of holy light.

## MEDITATIVE FOCUS

With closed eyes, see Jesus as a being of light with rays extending from every cell of his body. The light around his skin should appear as a luminous egg with golden rays or fibers extending everywhere into the universe. Imagine all of the great Christian presences—Mary, Francis, Hildegard, and all the other saints—standing next to Jesus. Each of them is also illuminated, and their holy rays of light interconnect with those of every other saint.

In your inner seeing, observe the fusion of all of these light rays as a way of knowing they are one source of light. When you have connected the light of these holy ones, you should see nothing but one powerful illumination.

Observe yourself walking toward this light and being lit up by it. The closer you get, the brighter you become. Experience your own rays of light connecting with the beams from all of the saints. Allow these connections

---

*As cited in Pappas, *Jesus' Tomb in India*, 148–49.

to pull your light into the central light of Jesus. Practice "lighting your-self" in many different ways over the months and years to come.

## LOST PARABLE: THE SACRED FIREFLY

In the beginning, God asked for light. A tiny insect, believing God was speaking directly to her, began emitting a bright, soft, intermittent glow of light. God smiled and was pleased with how the fly's faith and obedience had created a light for itself. God said to the little fly, "You shall be my sacred carrier of light. From this moment forward, creatures will know you as the sacred firefly. Your fire will remind others that the simplest of my creatures can be enlightened and carry the holy illumination."

Few of God's creatures were aware of the holy origin of the firefly. They took the light-emitting insect as a novelty, rather than as a holy teacher. The firefly wasn't recognized as holy until an old medicine man in South Dakota learned its holy nature through a great vision he had in the Black Hills.

This old man, Running Elk, was a believer in all religions. He participated in the old traditions of his people and was a member of several Christian churches. He prayed to Mecca every day and also practiced several Buddhist meditations. Running Elk was known to say, "I want to cover all the spiritual bases. Since you have to step on four different bases to hit a home run, I'm not going to take any chances with my spirituality." He made certain he always practiced at least four different spiritual traditions faithfully, one from each direction of the world.

One early spring evening, Running Elk was sitting on a hill making his prayers and holding a fast. A firefly came up to him and spoke these words: "I am going to tell you the story of how the Great Spirit gave me my name." The firefly told Running Elk what you just learned about the origin of its name and light, and went on to give him a gift:

*I want to give you my holy light. Since you have covered all the spiritual bases, it's time for you to carry the light. I will show you the medicine I carry for making light. You will learn how to pre-pare and carry it. In a special ceremony you will make this light fly. It will help open people's hearts and feed their faith in the great grandfathers and grandmothers. You must promise to keep yourself humble and not boast about the secret I am about to show you.*

The firefly then gave Running Elk the secret of making holy light. Running Elk carried the light in his old suitcase with all his other medicines, feathers, and rattles. When people asked him to feed their faith, he would arrange a dark room and ask them to pray with their hearts. If they were all sincere, the room would fill with the light of these sacred fireflies.

The ceremony of light became well known throughout the hills of South Dakota. People would travel great distances to have their faith fed by the holy lights. As their faith became stronger, miracles began taking place in the ceremonies. Sick people were healed and spiritual guidance was whispered into the ears of the faithful.

On a particular cold winter night long ago, a ten-year-old boy attended Running Elk's ceremony. When the room became dark the singers and drummers made music for the spirit lights. After their prayers, the sacred fireflies flew into the room. The boy, named Little Bear Thunder, felt someone tapping his shoulder. When he turned around he saw Buffalo Calf Woman standing behind him. She said, "Follow me. I will take you to the place of light." He reached out and held her hand. The two of them flew right through the ceiling into another world.

Everywhere Little Bear Thunder looked he saw beautiful light. Buffalo Calf Woman told him many things. She explained how he had entered the spirit world, where everyone is a light. She went on to speak these words:

*People only look like people on Earth because molecules and matter spin to create the illusion called "seeing." In the spirit world all molecules stop moving and come to complete stillness. In the absence of spinning, "seeing" disappears. All that remains is light that cannot be "seen" in the way earthlings understand sight. Here the light is felt by the inner eye and directly received by the spiritually opened mind.*

Then Buffalo Calf Woman told Little Bear Thunder the secret of the holy light:

*The secret involves getting the molecules—or what we call the "matter moles"—to stop spinning. The only way to do this on Earth is to exercise what you call "faith" through sincere prayer, singing, and dancing. When a group of people comes together as one and stops the spinning, the holy light appears. This is what the firefly taught Running Elk.*

At that instant Buffalo Calf Woman began to spin. As Little Bear Thunder observed her whirling movement, he heard her say:

*It looks like I'm starting to spin, but actually I'm slowing down my spin. You see me as a person only when I spin fast enough. As I slow down, you will see that I have always been spinning. When my movement comes to a rest, you will see who I really am.*

Sure enough, her spinning became slower and slower. She began getting smaller and smaller until, to Little Bear Thunder's great surprise, she became as small as a firefly. As she rested on his hand, he knew instinctively to lift her near his ear. She spoke these final words:

*I am the one who comes into the room when you people pray your faith. I am the holy light. Learn to stop the spinning and you will become a holy light. Then I will be able to tell you everything.*

Little Bear Thunder spent the rest of his life learning to slow down his spinning. He became a great holy man who had one simple practice— practicing the movement toward stillness.

He would go back and forth into the spiritual world learning from the sacred fireflies. Sometimes people attending his ceremonies would see the fireflies. They never knew he was one of the lights moving in the room. He kept that secret from everyone except his ten-year-old son, Singing Thunder.

Singing Thunder's story hasn't yet been told. He's still learning to slow down and become a light. We can report that Little Bear Thunder's last spoken words before he passed over were whispered to his son. He said something about a time when the fireflies would return to light up the black robe's religion. "The time has come for all faiths to be slowed down and lit up," he said. Those were his last words.

Ever since his father's death, Singing Thunder comes once a year to the place where Little Bear Thunder taught him about the holy light. The local people know when this takes place, because on that summer night, what seems to be an infinitude of fireflies fill the sky. That's when everyone is reminded of the power of the firefly's holy light.

## ACTIVE MYSTICAL PRACTICE

Choose a week to conduct the following practice. Keep track of the friends and colleagues you talked to during the week. In a notebook record a description of the moments in which you believe you were able to offer some light to another person's life. This light may be in the form of support, respect, enthusiasm, humor, or helpful knowledge. There are many ways of offering light to others. One way may even include sending good thoughts toward them.

At the end of the week reflect on how many people you gave light to and the various ways in which you gave them light. Purchase the same number of candles as the number of people you helped light. Arrange a time for a ceremony. Light the candles in a dark room and see the amount of light you put into the world in one week.

# 7

# THE NEW ENGLAND SHAKERS AND THE INDIAN SPIRITS

*This was a time of unusually vivid visions and violent shaking and whirling. . . . It was during this period that Indian ways crept into Shaker ritual. . . . Gifts flowed from the Indian spirits to the Shakers steadily until 1845. Directly after one of these exchanges, a display of lights was seen in the sky.*

JAMES W. MAVOR, JR. AND BYRON E. DIX,
*MANITOU: THE SACRED LANDSCAPE OF NEW ENGLAND'S NATIVE CIVILIZATION*

## CONTEMPLATION

In 1837 a wild revival of spiritual activity spread through many Shaker Church communities in New England. The Shakers, so named because of their shaking behavior, were well known for their ecstatic experiences. But at this time in their history, they began to enter the spiritual realms of their Indian neighbors. The characteristic experience usually began with involuntary shaking, jerking, spinning, and energetic body motions. Eventually going into trance, the seekers would sometimes have visions of Indians. While inspired, the recipient of such a vision would fall to the floor and become rigid, while the Indian spirits would gift them with images, songs, and revelations. One girl spoke in an Indian language and continued doing so for weeks after her trance.

Visions of Indians became common among the Shakers in the 1840s. Clairvoyant communication between one Shaker community and another occurred frequently, a spiritual phenomenon not unknown to the Indians. There were several well-documented cases of clairvoyant messages being sent between congregations in the state of New York. The Indian spirits presented the Shakers with the holy pipe and taught them that God was both a Father and Mother.

Shakers began purifying themselves with sweat baths. Meeting at sacred places in the woods, the Shakers would allow themselves to take in the spirits of many Indians. On top of a mountain at Hancock, Massachusetts, they held ceremonies that began with fasting, prayers, and the distribution of spiritual offerings. They then proceeded to walk up the mountain, singing and dressed in ornate clothing.

At the top of the mountain, the participants opened themselves to direction from the spirits. Everyone removed their coats and danced with high energy, sometimes leaping, skipping, clapping, and shouting. At a certain moment in the ceremony, spiritual seeds were distributed around a stone they called "the fountain." The people spiritually watered these seeds from pots they had carried with them. It was at this time that the Indian spirits would come into their presence. After some of these spirit encounters, the Shakers saw a display of lights in the sky.

Scholars later noted that the shamanic dances of the California Yurok were very similar to those danced in Shaker rituals. On the west coast of the United States, the shamanic practices of Indians and Christianity also blended in the group called the Indian Shakers. They danced a holy dance that anthropologist H. G. Barnett saw and described as similar to the sacred dance of the Holy Rollers of Appalachia and the New England Shakers.

Christianized Indians and "Indianized" Shakers spread throughout the Midwest in the seventeenth century. In every case, spirits would enter the body and cause it to move and shake. The movements became a circular dance that gave birth to visions and spiritual gifts ranging from revelation to healing. The most famous expression of this sacred dance is called the Ghost Dance. It led to such profound spiritual experiences that the United States government at that time made it illegal to perform.

Government agents forbade the Ghost Dance because of its "physical and mental effect on the participants." On November, 1890, Agent D. F. Royer telegraphed Washington, D. C., and expressed concern that the dance was making Indians go "wild and crazy," thus justifying the need for thousands of soldiers. In the same month the President of the United States ordered the Secretary of War to use the military to control the situation and limit any further outbreak of the dance. The subsequent ugly violence—the slaughter of American Indian women and children when they danced the Ghost Dance at Wounded Knee—is now history, a story not told enough in our schools or churches.

The Shakers, like the Indians, were also persecuted for their dance. In 1810, eighty years before the massacre at Wounded Knee, five hundred armed men and two thousand spectators attacked the Shaker community at Turtle Creek in southern Ohio. Barton Stone, the leader of the ambush, wrote that it was necessary to launch this assault because "they have made a shipwreck of our faith, and turned it aside to an old woman's fable."

The lesson is clear. It is no surprise that the shamanic expression of Christianity seems absent in our culture. Most if not all shamanic practices have been silenced and often attacked. Religions that have been reduced to vehicles for social and mental control do not want people dancing. In states of ecstasy, people may go "wild and crazy." Those who are committed to exercising authority over others simply cannot tolerate the bliss that leads to dancing in the fields. In the dance of Holy Communion with saints and spirits, all earthly authority is illuminated and seen to be nothing important. This is a dance that sets people free.

## MEDITATIVE FOCUS

In your mind, travel back in time to the early days, when the Shakers were active in New England. See them climbing the holy mountain with their blue and white garments and handbells. As they reach the top observe the wild movements that transform their weathered faces into the young faces of children. See them skipping and jumping with joy.

Hear them sing a song that brings them together in a large circle. They begin moving to the right and then to the left. Back and forth, the movement continues, bringing a trance to every dancer. One by one the dancers begin to whirl as they move to the right and then to the left. The circle appears to be one great entity that breathes, first to the right and then to the left. As the body of the Great Dancer pulses, breathing this way and that, a wind begins to blow upon each individual participant. Each Shaker is now still. Now it is the wind that moves them and creates the inner vision of a dance in motion. The danced bodies surrender their minds to the movement of the dancing wind until each individual collapses onto the ground. In their minds, they fall through the ground and enter another world. Here the wind takes them to the saints and spirits.

Imagine yourself as one of these dancing Shakers. You are in the spiritual world of the dancing wind. Any spirit or saint you wish to see will come if you simply ask. Jesus and Mary are available, as are all the saints and spirits of Christianized Indians and Indianized Christians. Allow the inner wind from the deepest part of you to dance you toward these holy presences and spiritual guides.

## LOST PARABLE: THE MYSTERIOUS CROSS AND DANCE OF THE MIRAMICHI

Sometime in the 1600s a Jesuit priest named Father Le Clercq took off on a great voyage. He sailed across the ocean and met up with the Miramichi Indians on the Gaspé Peninsula in eastern Canada. He met shamans who showed him how they communicated with spirits. Assisted by spiritual objects, they went into ecstatic states and were completely transformed. The spirits used the shaman's body and voice for expression. To his great surprise, Father Le Clercq discovered that the Indians already knew of Jesus from Nazareth.

Le Clercq actually wrote down a story told to him by the Miramichi Indians. A man once appeared to these Indians in their dreams and showed them a cross he was holding. He told them to make these crosses in order to heal illness. The Indians began making crosses and undertook no task without wearing them. Crosses are still found today in their burial places. In 1682, Father Emanuel Juneau arrived and declared the crosses had to be associated with Christian mission work. An elder corrected the priest, maintaining that the Indians had been making the crosses before the black robes ever stepped on their soil. Father Le Clercq also strongly insisted that the crosses were there long before the arrival of the Jesuits.

The black robes called these Indians "the cross-bearers." They decided that the crosses had nothing to do with Christianity and abandoned their efforts to convert any of the Indians along the Gaspé Peninsula, believing they were too resistant to the faith. They pulled out and went to the headwaters of the Saint Lawrence River. The Church was mystified that they gave up on these Indians because of Le Clercq's own admission in a letter that "the Gaspesians were the most docile of all the Indians of New France and most susceptible to the instruction of Christianity."*

What Le Clercq did not know was that Jesus and the wolves that accompanied him had visited these Indians. He had come to them in their dreams and showed them the four directions of the cross. During his visit they discussed the ancient Indian practice of fasting for a vision. They told him that when they entered the woods to undergo a fast, they sometimes encountered an *oiaron* or *manitou,* a personal spiritual guardian.

Jesus showed the Indians a dance that would enable them to encounter spirits in the same way they did on a vision fast. In this dance, they would begin by singing and clapping hands, allowing their bodies to get jolted and jerked around as the spirit tried to get into them. Once the spirit was inside their body, it danced them into states of ecstasy, allowing them to cross over into the spirit world. They would behold visions and sometimes be given the spiritual gifts of prophecy, healing, or vision for creating some work of art. Jesus told them how to dance the dance that would later be known among Shakers and Ghost Dancers. He also revealed to the Miramichi the story of how he learned to dance:

---

*Chrétien Le Clercq, *New Relations of Gasperia, with the Customs and Religion of the Gasperian Indians,* translated and edited by William F. Ganong. Champlain Society, 1910.

*A long time ago I went into the desert to fast and pray for guidance. Many temptations were offered, and my sincerity and steadfastness endured each challenge. On the night of the thirtieth day, an angel of light appeared to me and said she would teach me the secret of the firefly's light. She told me God gave the firefly its gift because of its faith. With the angel's help, the firefly then taught God to teach human beings to dance.*

*The angel of light then showed me a circle of people holding hands. All holy dancing moves around a circle, and making the circle dance requires two magical ingredients—a melody and a rhythm. What I learned in the desert was to chant and pipe so others could dance. Unless one dances, one cannot know what the dance can bring. When I pipe the music, the dancers enter the spiritual air. This cannot ever be known outside the experience of the holy movement.*

The art of dancing requires the ability to create different patterns of spinning. The most powerful dances are the circle dances. Melodies feed the longings of the mystical heart and set it free to soar above a doubting mind. At the same time, cadences of rhythm call the body to move and jump, loosening the bind of gravity. In this flight, music speaks a sacred truth and rides the pulse of rhythm.

Jesus and the Indians danced together in a holy ring dance. People were healed, given sacred guidance, and shown unspeakable mysteries. When Jesus left he reminded them that they now knew how to meet him in the dance. "I will show you something to make in a future dance. It will keep your faith strong." Those were the last words of Jesus to the Miramichi Indians. Years later they dreamed of a man holding a cross in his hands.

## ACTIVE MYSTICAL PRACTICE

With a group of friends, go to a woods or open field and gather some large stones. Make an inner circle of eight stones large enough to contain a fire. Around this circle, make a larger circle of twelve stones. These are the stones the dancers will move around, and the inner circle will hold the inner fire.

As evening falls, start a fire in the inner circle. There should be wood piled in all directions within the stone circle. When it becomes dark, stand around the outer circle stones and hold hands. Listen to the sound of the fire as if it were singing a song. Stomp the ground with your feet to create a rhythm using the Earth as your drum. Some of you may choose to wear bells around your ankles.

With time, the group will begin moving in a circle around the fire. Allow any sounds or movements to freely come forth and give them no interpretation or evaluation. Allow every dancer to become tuned to the dance. When dancers want to break away from the circle and move into their own space, allow this to take place naturally. Do not shape the dance or the ceremony. Let the dance shape your experience.

Know that people have danced spiritual ring dances since the beginning of human history. Jesus and the Indians, as well as the Bushmen in the Kalahari Desert and the Sufis in the Middle East, have danced and whirled themselves into great mysteries.

# 8

# THE PROVE:
# THE SHAMANIC USE OF
# THE HOLY BOOK

*All Scripture is inspired by God and profitable for teach-*
*ing, for reproof, for correction, for training in righteous-*
*ness; so that the man of God may be adequate, equipped*
*for every good work.*

2 TIMOTHY 3:16–17

## CONTEMPLATION

On the Caribbean island of St. Vincent, there are Christian shamans that were once known as Shakers. Much like the Shakers of New England, they were called that because of the way they would shake when the spirit came upon them. Today they call themselves Spiritual Baptists, but they still shake and shout for the Lord. They practice a mystical method of opening the Bible to find a scripture that will speak directly to them. This requires them to access a sincere and open attitude, pray for a scripture, and then open the Bible and pay attention to where their finger rests upon a page. They take that particular verse as proof of God's presence and direction.

There are a number of variations on the "prove." If an outsider claims to have spiritual authority, others can faithfully open the Bible and see what the scripture has to say. A practitioner who is trying to make an important decision or discern between choices of perspective may also utilize the prove. Keep this in mind: If the Holy Spirit is present during this practice, it has the power to direct you to a Bible verse that can help you. The objective is to enter into a holy state of mind and then open yourself to being moved by spirit. If you haven't appropriately prepared your attitude, the scriptural choice could be distorted by inner psychological conflict that might lead you astray. When conducting a prove, remember that its authority should be given credibility only on the basis of how pure your heart is when you open the holy book.

As I write, I will consult the scriptures to see what knowledge they bring us about this practice. First I pray that the readers of this book receive some messages that will direct their understanding of how to view this practice. As I open the Bible, it gives these words:

O ye simple, understand wisdom, and, ye fools, be ye of an understanding heart. (Proverbs 8:5)

Yes, we simple fools must be ready to receive wisdom and have an understanding heart. I invite you to ask for an understanding heart and to approach the Lord with me, asking sincerely, "What are we to do, dear Lord?" To the Bible we turn, again opening its pages:

Unto thee, O God, we give thanks, unto thee do we give thanks; for thy name is near thy wondrous works declare. (Psalms 75:1)

With this directive, please join me in giving thanks. Over and over again, we shall proclaim, "Thank you Lord! Thank you! Thank you!" In this thankful consciousness, we find ourselves even more prepared to open the book. We find:

The flowers appear on the earth, the time of the singing of birds is come, and the voice of the turtle is heard in our land. (Solomon 1:12)

This verse directs our mind to the beauty of the Earth and the value of song in thanking the Lord for all of creation. Let us now sing praise, encouraging our minds to become full of music, words surrendering to the lyrical movement of song. As we deepen our preparation to receive the Lord's teaching, I open the Bible in the midst of musical praise:

And his brethren also went and fell down before his face; and they said, Behold, we be thy servants. (Genesis 50:18)

This I take as a command. Let us fall down upon the ground and humbly proclaim ourselves to be holy servants. In this position of servitude, we again turn to the holy book, opening it carefully to find:

And straightway many were gathered together. Insomuch that there was no room to receive them, no, not so much as about the door; and he preached the word unto them. (Mark 2:2)

Let us hear and profoundly understand that we are not ready to receive the words of Jesus unless we have leveled ourselves to the ground. Only then, in purest humility and servitude, may our hearts have the capacity to receive holy teaching. I pray to our Savior, "Please, we ask as humble servants to receive your teaching. What must we learn this moment in our lives? We ask you with a heart that thirsts for your wisdom." We again approach the Bible, and sacred words come forth through another prove:

Behold, all ye that kindle a fire, that compass yourselves about with sparks that ye have kindled. This shall ye have of mine hand; ye shall lie down in sorrow. (Isaiah 50:11)

"Yes, Lord, we have kindled the fire by asking to serve your will. Please tell us more, so that our hearts may understand." We open the book again:

There is no fear in love; but perfect love casteth out fear: because fear hath torment. He that feareth is not made perfect in love. (John 4:18)

"Lord, we want to enter into your love. Please burn away all fear. Transform us into servants of your love. Make us instruments of perfect love." We ask for one more teaching. The Bible speaks its conclusion for today's practice of the prove:

> Therefore if any man be in Christ, he is a new creature; old things are passed away; behold, all things are become new. (2 Corinthians 5:17)

"Thank you Lord, for again making us new. We ask that we have the wisdom to see all things as new and to let old things pass away. We thank you."

This is a dynamic way in which we may learn from the holy book. We must strive to open our hearts, humble our presence in the greater scheme of all living beings, and carefully attend to the ways in which the Lord chooses to speak.

## MEDITATIVE FOCUS

You are dreaming. In this visionary place, you find an old man and an old woman waiting for you inside a library. There is only one book and it is gigantic, as large as a fisherman's net. To see it you must walk over to a balcony and look down. It rests below with its pages open like outstretched arms. The old woman speaks to you:

> *You must have faith and jump into its arms. If you have fear, you will fall through its pages and keep falling throughout the rest of time. If you have any anger, jealousy, or greed in your heart, its pages will turn to steel and you will be hurt when you fall. On the other hand, if you are sincere, full of love for all beings, something special will take place. It will gently catch you, like a soft pillow. When you land upon it, you will fall asleep upon a particular scripture. In this sleep you will dream a holy dream, and a voice will speak the scripture that has embraced you. This scripture will become your wisdom. Carry it with you so that it may continue to bring you comfort and peace. Allow it to give meaning to your life.*

In this meditation, bring yourself to the edge of the balcony. Make your-self ready for the jump. Allow your heart-filled mind to carry you forth.

## LOST PARABLE: REVEREND WARREN, THE POINTER OF ST. VINCENT

Warren was unable to walk and he never learned to read. Yet that didn't stop him from becoming one of the greatest spiritual leaders of a dreamy Caribbean island. Warren loved Jesus and never stopped having dreams about the stories in the Bible. He also seemed to have a natural intuition about what was going on with other people. He could tell someone what their children were doing, even if they hadn't heard from them for several years. He simply knew things.

More importantly, Warren claimed to talk to Jesus and Mary, along with most of the saints. Though illiterate, he could tell you everything about God's love and the mysteries of the spiritual world. What he was famous for was the way in which he could open the Bible and point to a scripture that would speak directly to a person who came to him for help. No one knew how he did it, and not everyone accepted Warren's explanation. He would say, "If you love God and ask him to direct you, it will happen. The same is true for my finger when I point to a verse. You see, God takes my hands, opens the good book, and points my finger at what you need to hear. I can't read, but I don't need to. God directs my hands and my voice and my dreams."

And so it happened that a group of theologians from Europe and America came to visit "Reverend Warren," as he was sometimes called, even though he had no formal education. He was, as his neighbors said, "ordained by the Holy Spirit." When the scholars introduced themselves to Warren, he started singing "Jesus Loves Me." He wouldn't stop singing. No one was able to ask a single question. All they heard was this simple song.

The next morning they returned and Reverend Warren was wait-ing for them. He had a large Bible resting on his lap, and he told them each to ask it questions. He didn't want any of their questions, he said, but told them to address all their inquiries to the Lord's words. And so they asked questions, one after another, and Reverend Warren opened the Bible and pointed to scriptures. They submitted even their most important theological questions, those they had devoted their lives to addressing. All questions were answered.

This went on for more than a week, until the theologians had exhausted all their questions. Reverend Warren again started to sing, "Yes, Jesus loves me." On and on he sang, as the theologians thanked him one last time before departing for home. They were so amazed they were unable to speak to one another. They flew home in silence. When they showed up for their next faculty meetings and classes, they remained silent. They were dumbstruck by the power of Reverend Warren's proves. Instead of talking, they began to open books and point to sentences or paragraphs. They did this with all of the world's holy books and found that they could not stop themselves from doing it. They stopped reading. They only pointed. Others marveled at how their fingers led them to words that would make a difference in other people's lives.

One by one, each theologian grew old, retired, and moved to the Caribbean. They each took only one book in their suitcase. They had all become true teachers who pointed the way for others.

## ACTIVE MYSTICAL PRACTICE

On a nightly basis, practice preparing yourself to be a receptacle of the Holy Spirit, asking it to use your hands to open the Bible and point to a scripture. When you read the scripture, honestly ask yourself whether it speaks to you or whether you did not get a good connection to the spirit. Assume that all scriptures that do not have an immediate impact on you are the result of improper tuning of your spiritual reception. Keep opening the Bible until you get a scripture that truly touches your heart. It must be a direct spiritual hit.

Keep a journal of each scripture that strikes you in this way. Over time, you will have an important collection of scriptures brought down by the spirit. Consider this your private collection of spiritual medicines. When the book is full, use it whenever you need to make an important decision or need help with some challenge in your life. Prepare yourself and then open the book, pointing to one of your spiritual medicines.

## 9

# RECEIVING THE STAFF AND OTHER SHAMANIC INSTRUMENTS

*Yea, though I walk through the valley of the shadow of death, I will fear no evil; For You are with me; Your rod and Your staff, they comfort me.*

PSALM 23:4

## CONTEMPLATION

When a shaman has a vision and is shown a sacred object, he or she may decide to go find the object in the physical world or make it for themselves. Anything seen in sacred vision may be brought into the physical plane and used as a shamanic tool or instrument. Some say these vision-inspired objects have sacred power. Perhaps it is more accurate to say that these gifts from the world of spirit boost the relationship of the shaman with the spirit world. Seeing or touching the object brings about a memory of the inspired vision which, in turn, recharges the shaman and fills him or her with great emotion and passion. In this way, the objects serve as links or bridges between imagination and realization.

When Christian shamans dream and vision sacred objects, they may choose to own and use them in their spiritual practice. It is best not to lust for spiritual objects. You may get what you ask for, and the cost is the responsibility to take care of these gifts and honor their entry into your world. Spiritual gifts are both a resource and a burden. They must be fed with prayers and offerings. Over the years, Christian shamans have been gifted with many different kinds of spiritual instruments that they use in their prayer, healing, and contemplative practices. For example, I have known shamans who received special crosses, beads, altars, pieces of wood, bells, colored designs, and even a shepherd's staff.

## MEDITATIVE FOCUS

Christian shamans are sometimes given a staff in a sacred dream. This dream is often taken to mean that one is being called to shepherd others in a spiritual way. After having such a dream, one is spiritually permitted to go find a staff. It may be a full-sized staff or a miniature one that you can keep in your pocket or purse.

For this meditation, create the image of a staff in your mind. Imagine your eyes slowing tracing its outline from top to bottom. Slowly and surely, allow yourself to visually inspect this staff. Do this over and over. See the staff as a dark color, but as you focus on it, allow the staff to become lighter. Eventually the staff should turn white, like a shining light. Cultivate this image in your meditative practice. See it as a way to prepare yourself to receive a sacred staff. If you receive the staff in a dream, privately refer to yourself as a newly initiated shepherd.

## LOST PARABLE: DREAMING THE STAFF

Years ago a young nursing student dreamed of a staff. It was made of wood and was painted white. In the dream, it floated across the room and landed in her hand. The next day she went to an art gallery and noticed a painting of a woman holding a staff. She thought of her dream and began wondering what it meant for her to see a staff. She thought about how a shepherd's staff can be used to direct sheep and how the curved end can be used to pull a sheep forward. She also imagined how a staff could be used to chastise a disobedient sheep. And finally, she thought of how a shepherd holds a staff to lead her sheep to green pastures, fresh water, and back to the fold in the evening.

That night she fell asleep thinking about the shepherd's staff she had seen the night before. Was it the staff of another shepherd pulling her in? Was it a gift to help her become a spiritual shepherd? She fell asleep wondering. To her surprise, she had another dream about the staff. It was still white, but this time it was small and fit inside the palm of her hand. The tiny staff was vibrating with a kind of rippling energy. She started to squeeze the staff in her palm, and then she woke up.

For a week, she wondered about the palm-sized staff. She wished the dream had lasted longer. She could not stop thinking about the tiny staff.

She decided to tell her grandmother about these dreams. Her grandmother was an unusual woman who others believed had spiritual gifts. She filled her cupboards and walls with unusual objects and pictures that no one understood. Grandmother's house had a special feeling to it, and it felt good to be around her. When her grandmother heard about these dreams, she cried out with excitement. "Yes, granddaughter, that is very important. The Lord is giving you a staff. All you have to do is make it and hold on to it every night. It will bring forth the energy of the Holy Ghost. I know, because I have one of those staffs." As she spoke, she went to her dresser and pulled out a box. Inside the box was a paperclip that had been bent into the shape of a staff. Grandmother had painted it red. On its top she had attached a tiny ribbon.

"Here's my staff. Try it out." The young nursing student reached out for the staff. When she squeezed it, she could remember all the time she had spent with her grandmother. It filled her with much love, and a tingle of energy shot through her body. Grandmother could see that she understood what the staff was for and immediately said, "Now it's time to make your staff. There is no right way to make it. You must simply do it yourself. Any way is fine, as long as you are the one who makes it."

The young woman went home and privately made her own staff, which she now holds every night. She is still holding it, feeling the love for all the shepherds in her life, using its energy to direct others who need help and guidance. She learned that the staff brings her home, and also helps her bring others to their rightful place in the world.

## ACTIVE MYSTICAL PRACTICE

Consider the fact that anything you see or hear in a sacred vision is an invitation to receive a spiritual gift. To draw what you see or sing the song you hear brings the sacred into the everyday world. The shaman becomes an expert at crossing the boundary between spirit and material worlds. Contemplate having one object to keep by your side to enhance and inspire your spiritual life. Do not ask for it, but imagine how it could help you move further along on your spiritual journey.

When you have imagined this object, open your Bible and write down the name of the object on the page that is opened. Keeping the Bible open, place it by the side of your bed. See the name of your imagined object as "spiritual bait" intended to bring down a sacred dream. Before going to bed, set your mind in a good place by reading the one verse on the opened page that has the most meaning to you. Continue doing this every night until you catch a dream that you believe is sacred for you. Believe that the sacred dream empowers the name of the imagined object and the chosen scripture to be even more effective as spiritual bait the next time you choose to go spiritually fishing.

# 10

# THE SHAMANIC
# POWER OF LOVING
# ONE'S ENEMY

*Love your enemy, do good to those who hate you.*

LUKE 6:27

*Why should you love your enemy? In order that you may
bring the healing rays of your love into his dark, hatred-
stricken heart. . . . Thus will the flame of your love burn
the partitions of hatred and misery which separate your
Soul from other Souls and all Souls from the vast sea of
Infinite Love.*

PARAMHANSA YOGANANDA

## CONTEMPLATION

Many people became upset with Jesus because he refused to fuel the fires
of justly provoked anger and retribution. There is no doubt that we all
witness the cruelty and wrongdoings of other human beings. When this
action is directed toward us or toward the ones we love, it is very difficult not to become angry or filled with the hateful desire to strike back
in the name of justice. Jesus shocked and even angered those around him
when he suggested that we not lift an angry arm, but open a loving hand

to our enemies and to those who would do us harm. He came to replace the Old Testament law with New Testament love.

The arm of hate too easily falls prey to the belief that it cannot be satiated until the perceived enemy is destroyed. This is how agents of justice transform themselves into the same evil that they oppose. Refusing to feed hate and outrage is the first step toward extinguishing it in others. We feed the evil in our opponent when we participate in any tactics of destruction. Jesus invited us instead to move to a higher ground.

Loving one's enemy is not simply a tactic to conquer the opponent with love. It is an understanding that lifts us out of the temptation to judge the differences between ourselves and others. Instead, we can view every other person's conduct as a different aspect of our own being. We can learn to see ourselves in everyone else, including those who appear ready to destroy us. Healing another becomes a powerful way to heal oneself. The action of love toward the vicious other is thus no less than an attempt to heal oneself and the other by dissolving the difference that separates us.

There is no more powerful medicine than the practice of loving our enemy. The extent to which we are outraged is a measure of the transformative power that will be released when we surrender to the healing response of love. No potion, talisman, incantation, or spiritual ally can come close to the Earth-shaking power of the shamanic practice of loving those who are most difficult to love. This is where the heart becomes an instrument of alchemy and transforms noxious odors into nectars of the gods. Here darkness is turned into the golden rainbow body of luminous wisdom.

## MEDITATIVE FOCUS

Think of the person in your life you feel is most likely to do you or your family harm. Picture them throwing sharply pointed arrows at your home. As they do this, see yourself sitting in the center of your home, remembering all times your heart has been filled with love, wonder, and appreciation for the miracle of life. Think of a beautiful stream in the woods or the day your baby was born. Remember seeing someone help another person when they didn't have to, or hearing that someone in trouble was blessed with some good luck, and so forth. As you fill your heart in this way, know that your house is being surrounded by a golden light.

When the arrows enter this golden light, see them dissolve. See these arrows feed the light and make it brighter. Notice how the attacks of the other's arrows make the light around your home shine brighter and brighter. Believe that this truly happens and imagine ways in which you could learn to be thankful to those who are your enemies. Silently thank them for helping to bathe your home in pure, bright, golden light.

## LOST PARABLE: PRAYING FOR A GOOD ENEMY

There was once a quiet man who never had an enemy. He was so at peace with his life that he fell into a deep sense of relaxation. Unfortunately, he was unable to stay awake. Wherever he went, he fell asleep.

As a result of this condition, he lost his job. No one wanted to be around him and he was eventually left all alone. Having nowhere to go, he walked into a great forest. Lying down peacefully under a tall oak tree, he fell asleep. In his dreams a fox came to him and said, "Why don't you go find yourself a good enemy? You're wasting your life with this peaceful slumber. Wake up and set out on a great expedition to find an enemy."

The fox in the man's dream made him uncomfortable. He could no longer sleep. Upset by the dream, he decided he could not argue with its message. In some way it had set forth a seed of truth. To his surprise, he decided to follow the fox's advice.

Off he went, traveling throughout the world in search of a good enemy. Wherever he went, he failed at getting anyone angry. He would sometimes beg people to hate him. He even tried to pay a criminal to be his enemy. What happened time and time again is that everyone was entertained by his action and requests. As hard as it may be to believe, this man could not find himself an enemy!

The fox came more and more often to his dreams and would make fun of him for his unsuccessful efforts. The man even dreamed that he had a fight with the fox about the way he had disrupted his life. The very next morning he realized he had truly found his enemy—it was the fox in his dreams.

With this insight he was able to work vigorously through each day while waiting to dream of wrestling with the fox during his evening slumber. The fox brought him a new sense of being awake and fully alive. He eventually acquired a good job, married a good woman, and raised a healthy family. All of this helped him fall asleep every night and get at that fox. The fox had been right. He needed an enemy in order to have an awakened life. And he had found a good enemy.

For the next ten years the man wrestled with the fox every night in his dreams. Then it happened that another creature, an otter, came into his dreams and told him that the fox was not real. It was his dream and therefore was a part of himself. The man could no longer wrestle with the fox. He stopped having an enemy and his life began to lose its zest and vitality. Months went by with the man grieving over the loss of his enemy. The fox, who now had become a friend, tried to comfort the man in his dreams. One night the fox said, "You should be angry with that otter. He's the one who messed things up." And so the man started wrestling with the otter every night. His vitality and zest for life again returned.

With time the otter became his friend. One by one he wrestled and became friends with every living creature on the Earth. In so doing, he learned something profound: He not only needed an enemy to empower his life, he needed one to assure that he would acquire a new friend. However, with each conversion of an enemy into a friend, he was left in need of a new enemy. He learned that he could never live free of an enemy. He did not want to risk going back to sleep and losing the vitality he now cherished. He learned a deeper way of appreciating and loving the contribution that his enemies made to his life.

## ACTIVE MYSTICAL PRACTICE

Purchase a picture book of animals. Before going to bed every evening, randomly open the book to a picture of a particular animal. Imagine a person who is actually your enemy that the animal reminds you of and what they would be like if they were to turn into the animal and become your enemy on that plane of existence. Then stare at the animal's picture for five minutes and wonder whether it will wrestle with you in your dreams. Keep doing this until you dream of the animal. When you dream of it, cut the picture out of the book and place it under your bed. Do this until you have dreamed of wrestling every animal in the book. One by one all the animals will find their place under your bed. Appreciate how working with the image of an animal makes it easier to tame an actual enemy in your life.

# 11

# SOUL-MAKING MUSIC

*Rejoice in the Lord, O you righteous!*
*Praise befits the upright.*
*Praise the Lord with the Lyre,*
*make melody to him with the harp of ten strings!*
*Sing to him a new song,*
*play skillfully on the strings, with loud shouts.*

PSALM 33:1–3

## CONTEMPLATION

The soul does not speak with words, nor does it listen to most speech. Its language is music. The language most like music is poetry, a verbal approximation of music. Musicians and a few poets come closest to understanding the logic and mind of the soul. I once heard an old blues musician from Mississippi say that the most dangerous and revolutionary act on Earth is to turn people on to music. He proposed that if everyone had some mastery of a musical instrument, the world surely would be a different place.

Society and its educational institutions have done everything possible to make certain that very few of us master a musical instrument. This assures restricted access to the deepest levels of soulful being. Obedience to authoritative structures diminishes when confronted with rhythmic and melodic soul making. A conspiracy has been leveled against us. Its rhetoric elevates the importance of property rights, capital, status, employment, and college test scores. It actually has everything to do with blocking the main road to our soul.

Jesus knew this would happen, so he took the time to plant seeds of poetry and music in the Earth, insuring that future generations would have keys to open the celestial kingdoms. It was even rumored that the second coming would involve a return of music and poetry to the silent voices and deaf ears that had been imprisoned by logics of law and reason. This we know because of the ways in which music and poetry continue to disturb, liberate, arouse, impassion, lift, and shape the soul.

## MEDITATIVE FOCUS

Imagine that you and everyone you know have been magically granted mastery of at least one musical instrument. You are able to play any music that enters your mind and enjoy composing for those occasions that touch you emotionally. See how the expression of music might change everything in your life. Hear yourself humming the music you would make. Imagine having dreams filled with music and sharing that music with all of your friends. See the world populated with as many music stores as there are groceries and as many music halls as there are churches and stadiums. Pretend that government as we now know it no longer exists. Instead of a president, we would have a national conductor or musical director. Instead of legislative, executive, and judicial branches, we would have branches of rhythm, melody, and harmony. Begin thinking how one might overthrow government with music.

## LOST PARABLE: THE FIRST NOTE

Once upon a time someone sang the first note of music. When others heard it, no one was able to speak anymore. Speaking was a pale force

compared to the beauty and power of song. The world became populated with singing voices. People and birds became best friends.

It wasn't long before the birds taught humans how to make musical
instruments. Now the singing of the birds and people was accompanied
by great orchestras and ensembles. God was very happy with the sound
of creation heard in every spot of the world.

Due to agents of early papal propaganda, the story of Adam and Eve
has been somewhat distorted. Adam and Eve never got into trouble for
taking an apple. They became troubled because they were introduced
to the difference between *should* and *should not*. Before the introduc-
tion of this distinction by God and the long slash known as the serpent,
there were no "should nots." Everything was connected, and all action
nurtured all parts of the whole. When God and the serpent of distinction
introduced the difference between should and should not, Adam and
Eve started to question whether they should eat the sacred apple fruit,
a delicious and most wholesome contribution to their health and the
health of the whole ecosystem.

They became confused, and it was this seed of confusion, not the
seed of an apple, that led to all the trouble that came afterward. Eventually, this led to a conspiracy against music. Because of the fall in the
garden, it wasn't long before people began to argue that if anything feels
good, tastes good, sounds good, or looks good, then it must be wrong
and a bad temptation. Music became one of the forbidden apples.

This upset God. The Great Spirit had made a mistake in having
introduced the slash of distinction. It was an error that began splitting
everything apart—day and night, good and bad, health and illness,
work and play, and even God was divided into two parts, Satan and
the rest of God that was left after Satan was subtracted. This led to the
wars of difference that have plagued our planet ever since that original
split.

God tried to fix this mess by sending a Holy Son of Light, the one we
call Jesus. Unfortunately, Jesus forgot to bring his musical instruments
and became a great storyteller and shaman instead. Although his stories
and shamanic encounters were not enough to complete all the necessary changes, he started a soulful revolution. He quietly planted seeds of

music and poetry and saw to it that the world became more bountiful with the melodic fruit of each passing generation.

In the middle of Jerusalem is a drum with a piece of papyrus inside it. The message on it was transcribed by an old scholar who immediately gave up his university appointment upon deciphering its meaning. The words stated:

> *I will reappear in the future on a concert stage during the annual Grammy Awards. I'll bring my music so that the revolution of soul making can be fully launched. It will be another resurrection. Those who thought I was blind, will hear that I see, and those that think I am gone, will feel I'm here.*
>
> *Bring it on,*
> *Brother Ray*

The scholar became a soulful musician and shared the secret message only with other musicians who ate at least one apple a day.

## ACTIVE MYSTICAL PRACTICE

Keep a fresh apple on your desk. Purchase the sheet music of one of your favorite songs. Cut out a few notes from this music and rest it on top of your apple. Know that your apple holds the note that can be sounded to initiate the beginning of foot-stomping, hand-clapping soul making.

When the time is right and you feel so moved, bring forth the song through singing, humming, or playing a recording. Dance to it while holding the apple. Dance the apple. Imagine it singing. Don't eat this apple until you have taped the stem to the notes of music. Let that stem be a reminder of how music is a link to your soul. If you don't eat the apple, give it to someone who will.

# 12

# THE PILGRIMAGE
# TO SILENCE

*We are subjected to an intensity and consistency of noise*
*that is absolutely unprecedented in human experience,*
*and we don't even take note of it. . . . Spend at least two*
*minutes making a mental list of the things you hear at this*
*moment. Now imagine that number multiplied by a factor*
*of about 5,000. This is the amount of noise you endure*
*every day.*

C. W. McPherson, *Keeping Silence:*
*Christian Practices for Entering Stillness*

*But the Lord is in his holy temple: let all the earth keep*
*silence before him.*

Habakkuk 2:20

## CONTEMPLATION

The deepest entry into Christian Shamanism takes place after you leave
the words of holy scripture, teachers, and even your own inner voice
behind. After the words comes a great silence. This silence attracts the
manifestation of a great, warm, and holy white light. It fills you with a
knowing that stills all words while electrifying every sensory vessel. Here

you find the heart of your spiritual pilgrimage. With this home of light, every day launches a unique spiritual journey that leads you back to your evening roots. Then you discover that every day is a whole life, an opportunity for fully coming into the pilgrimage of your soul.

## MEDITATIVE FOCUS

See a sky filled with every word that has ever been written and spoken. One by one, each word dissolves into a cloud until only one word is left in the sky. This word is *still*. Watch each letter—*s, t, i, l,* and *l*—become smaller and smaller until they are small dots. Turn each dot into a raindrop and allow them to fall to the ground. After the rain falls, listen to how the world sounds when all the words are gone.

## LOST PARABLE: THE ALTAR
## OF SILENCE

A nine-year-old girl once went to church and during a prayer heard a scratching sound underneath her feet. When she looked at the floor there was a small church mouse waving her to come closer. She bent over and the mouse asked her to crawl underneath the pew the next time there was a prayer. Since everyone's eyes would be closed, she wouldn't have to worry about being seen.

When the minister prayed again, the little girl practically threw herself beneath the church pew. She found the mouse holding onto a tiny lever, and within a second, that mouse pulled the lever, releasing the whole floor. Down and down the little girl traveled as if she were Alice in Wonderland. "How can this be?" she asked out loud. "Am I in a dream?"

With a soft whoosh she landed in the middle of a giant white pillow. Wherever she looked she saw clouds. The mouse, now with little angel wings, floated over to her and remarked, "You thought you fell, didn't you? But you haven't fallen, you've risen into the world of angels."

"Why am I here?" the little girl asked. She heard a tapping sound, and then a whole chorus of mice angels began singing a most magnificent reply. Although she hadn't noticed them before, they now all appeared in a circle around her, each with a ring of light perfectly outlining its face. In their song, the mice explained that she had fallen into a very still and quiet place in her mind. She had not walked through the door of sleep, but by some great miracle had entered a spot in her mind that was both completely quiet and full of sound.

The mice angels taught the girl many wonderful things about spirit. She was given special instructions on how to return to this place whenever she felt the need to do so. Over the years the little girl looked forward to going to church and disappearing under the pew whenever the minister offered a prayer. Although her visits to the under-the-pew-world seemed like hours, days, and sometimes longer, she always found herself returning to the church pew at just the moment the minister was saying, "Amen."

And so it was that a little girl entered the kingdom of God by listening to a church mouse, who invited her to fall through the floor so that she might journey to the place of the great quiet where everything is heard. In that silence, she learned to hear for the first time.

## ACTIVE MYSTICAL PRACTICE

Spend a day looking for the quietest place you can find. Return to that place the following week. Sit there in silence and pretend that a tiny creature invited you to fall into the Earth and find a place of absolute stillness. There you will be able to hear one sentence that will totally change your life. Fantasize what that sentence would be. Go home, and without deliberation, slowly and carefully write down the sentence with the hand you do not normally use to write with. Place this sheet of written words underneath your pillow when you sleep. Before going to bed, tell yourself, "I'm now going to fall into that place of quiet and hear what lies beneath my pillow." Tell no one about the experiences that happen to you as a result of this practice. Be very still about it, even to your own inquiring mind. If you don't remember any dreams, be thankful that your inner silence has quieted its deepest teaching.

# 13

# REBIRTHING OUT
# OF THE GREAT
# MOTHER SEA

*Jesus answered, "Verily, verily, I say unto thee, Except a man be born of water and of the Spirit, he cannot enter into the kingdom of God."*

JOHN 3:5

## CONTEMPLATION

An ancient teacher once told a gathering of shamans that we each must be birthed at least twice in this lifetime. He spoke these words:

*The first time we are born through our mother's womb. The second time, we must be birthed through the spiritual waters of the Great Mother Sea. The Great Mother Sea is the originating source, the place from which all water flows and returns. This second birth is the baptism that marks entry into the spiritual forms.*

After this, the ancient teacher never spoke another word.

## MEDITATIVE FOCUS

Imagine five sincere seekers of spiritual truth spending twelve minutes a day in a special place where they simply utter the name of the Great Mother Sea. Believe that they were told that this is a way to begin their second birth. In your mind, join with them in the uttering of this sacred name. Imagine the ocean as you utter this name. See mermaids calling you to return to a mythical home that you accept as your place of origin. Go back through the great chain of being, passing through all the living forms, until you become a fish in the Great Mother Sea. Practice seeing and experiencing this imaginary devolution as a way of being more related to all of God's creation. Visualize all the living animals, the great chain of being, and pass through all its forms, going all the way back to the sea.

## LOST PARABLE: BECOMING THE GREAT MOTHER

A young girl once gave birth to a pregnant woman who announced that she was being born to bring forth the girl's mother. "How can I give birth to someone who will give birth to my mother?" the girl asked. Without hesitation, the mother of her mother responded, "So that you may become the Great Mother and begin your way back to the sea."

When the girl helped her daughter birth her mother, she became the Great Mother of the Sea and found her way back to the originating water. When she plunged into the sea, she became a mermaid and instantly understood all the mysteries of life. The greatest mystery that cannot be completely revealed hints at what this birthing and rebirthing has to do with the birth of Jesus. It suggests that you need to begin the process of birthing your mother. When talking about this birth, make sure to discuss it in a way that is never clearly understood. Say little about it, as is being done in the description you are now reading. Otherwise, the shock brought about by its complete revelation could precipitate a miscarriage. Please do not attempt to interfere with anyone's attempt to birth her mother and the subsequent pilgrimage to the Great

Mother Sea. Again, any story or discussion about these matters must be kept obscure so that it will help impregnate those who are willing to open themselves to its unspoken truth.

## ACTIVE MYSTICAL PRACTICE

See all living creatures as pregnant. Imagine they are pregnant with the child that will give birth to their own mother.

When it is near Mother's Day, purchase as many Mother's Day cards as you can find and send them to everyone you know. Sign each card with this signature: "The Great Mother Sea." Pretend that you will become one month more pregnant with each Mother's Day when you perform this task. After nine years of Mother's Days, get ready to dream about your own spiritual rebirthing in the Great Mother Sea. When the dream arrives, honor it with the placement of an image of a mermaid in your bedroom. Write these words on it: "In honor of the Great Mother Sea."

# 14

## UNLESS YE
## BECOME LIKE
## CHILDREN

*If any man among you thinks that he is wise in this age,*
*let him become foolish that he may become wise.*

1 CORINTHIANS 3:18

## CONTEMPLATION

Jesus was once asked what was most essential to know in order to become admitted to the mystical kingdom. He responded, "Unless ye become like children, you will never be admitted to my playground." Some shamans say these are the most important words ever spoken by him.

Contemplate the way in which these words celebrate a child's way of knowing. Think about how difficult it would be for an overly serious adult or scholarly theologian to accept that Jesus talked about a playground. Now pretend that you actually believe that Jesus spoke these words, and allow this belief to encourage you to become childlike with your spiritual practice.

## MEDITATIVE FOCUS

Fantasize seeing the faces of many children and visualize that the Creator is looking at these faces with you. Now imagine that all creative acts are mysteriously derived from an unconscious viewing of this scene. Pause, take a slow breath, and see that the Creator is one with this image. Propose to yourself that this view is the entrance to the holy kingdom.

## LOST PARABLE: HOLY SILLIES

One day God told Jesus a secret and commanded that he was never to tell it to any adult. "The kingdom of heaven is a place where everyone participates in the creation of holy sillies," God said. "A holy silly is pure merriment, silliness, ridiculousness, and playfulness." Jesus learned that he was sent to Earth not to die for people's sins, but to die for their over-seriousness. No one would understand this except for children. What adults saw as sin was to God an example of over-seriousness gone awry.

Jesus saw a future in which people would argue over everything in the Bible to such an extent that they would get mean about their differences and disagreements. This would lead to fighting, bitterness, righteousness, selfishness, and all the other forms of over-seriousness. He and God knew that the Bible was written in such a way that only children would know how to identify what was important. They did this by making sure that most Bibles had the words of Jesus printed in red ink. All children, before being influenced by education and training, would immediately recognize that those are the words that really matter. The most important truths are conveyed through the red letters. Every thing else is black and white background.

Few adults remember that the Bible is principally about the red-letter words. Even fewer remember that before they could read, they had encountered a Bible somewhere in their dreams that contained only these words, written in pure rainbow colors: "Unless ye become like children."

## ACTIVE MYSTICAL PRACTICE

Have a business card made that simply says, in multicolored ink:

UNLESS YE BECOME
LIKE CHILDREN

Place this card in as many Bibles as you can find—in hotel rooms, churches, chapels, religious bookstores, and so forth. See yourself as an evangelist of the most basic truth. Encourage others to join you in this crusade.

# Part II
# THE LOST
# DIRECTIVES

# INTRODUCTION TO
# THE LOST DIRECTIVES
## Meeting the Challenges of
## Everyday Life

*Verily I say unto you, Except ye turn, and become as little children, ye shall in no wise enter into the kingdom of heaven.*

MATTHEW 18:3

The lost teachings help us dig deep into furthest mind. They provide a means for creating the vertical pole of the four-cornered cross. As the imagination surrenders and plunges more deeply into fantasy and created story, an opposite outcome takes place simultaneously. As you go deeper into fantasy, you go higher into spiritual truth. This is because the vertical pole extends both ways, up and down. Similarly, as you go higher into spiritual truth, you will also find yourself traveling deeper into fantasy. The two opposites, spiritual fantasy and spiritual truth, are inseparable. Go far in one direction and find yourself going farther in the other. This is the secret of the four-cornered shamanic cross. It finds its strength in the marriage of opposites.

To make a shamanic cross, you also need the horizontal pole. This pole traverses the Earth and brings us to the ground of everyday experience, the essence of the human condition. In the everyday, we confront challenges, difficulties, dilemmas, problems, symptoms, nightmares, and suffering. The Christian shaman does not run away from the daily offerings of life's challenges. Nor does the Christian shaman directly attack them in a naive effort to rid the world of suffering. As Mother Teresa taught, suffering is God's gift to us. It is presented to guide, teach, and help us become transformed. Some believe this means that we are to wallow in our pain or surrender to a bleak view of life. Christian shamans, however, know that it is an invitation to create another shamanic pole, a horizontal pole that completes the construction of the sacred cross.

When suffering arrives in our life, we can be easily seduced into becoming overly serious about its presence. We worry what we should do about it, and we fret over how to get rid of the pain it causes us. Christian shamans instead greet and embrace the suffering. They play with it, doing so with the spirit of a child. As the Christian shaman meets daily problems and difficulties with absurdity, frivolity, and out right foolish behavior, a horizontal pole starts to stretch across the horizon.

Here lies another secret of shamanic tricksters, no matter where they live in the world. They meet seriousness with absurdity and comedic improvisation. In so doing, they are able to stretch suffering into a pole of opposites, with seriousness and absurdity resting on either end of the pole. This pole, stretched between the extremes of serious concern and fanciful play, creates energy and life.

I say to all that the lost teachings are only half of what you need to become a Christian shaman. You must also be introduced to the lost directives. They prescribe ways of making the horizontal arms of the shamanic cross. I will try to remember the words of one of my friends, an old alchemist. His teaching may help prepare you to be more willing and able to plunge into the most serious experiences of your life with an attitude of sacred lunacy and nonsense. Consider these thoughts as a preparation for making the horizontal pole of the cross:

*Your world, a place where shamans have been forgotten, is drowning in seriousness—serious problems, serious solutions, and serious understandings. Most people have become too adult, at the cost of throwing away the imaginative resources of childhood. As serious participants in the consensual non-shamanic cultural reality, people find that normal difficulties may, over time, become a form of sinking quicksand. Taking everyday difficulties to a professional expert may even make things worse. More often than not, they can contribute to making the situation even more serious by pronouncing a psychological label or suggesting that there are repressed traumatic experiences just beneath the surface. When your difficulties and challenges are taken that seriously, you may easily be led down the path of becoming a professional patient with a locked-in symptom, forever following the routine of getting pills and psychological explanations. In this state, you will find it nearly impossible to know the horizontal pole of the shamanic cross.*

*All wise shamans, Christian as well as others, recognize that the key to entering the spiritual kingdom is to first enter the child's mind. Consequently, they do not get overly serious about existential challenges, difficulties, and dilemmas. Being too serious takes away your spiritual arms, leads you away from the desired kingdom, and points you straight to existential hell. The Christian shaman walks away from inappropriate over-seriousness and returns to the playful spirit of a child. That's when the world of personal freedom, creative expression, and trickster presence reopens. Here the spiritual arms are brought forth, enabling spiritual hands to freely create and participate in the world.*

The following signs indicate that you may be stuck in the quicksand of too much seriousness. They indicate that your childlike spirit is not fully operational, a danger for the Christian shaman.

1. You spend too much time worrying about a problem, and do not devote enough time to play, frivolity, absurdity, and laughter.
2. You spend too much money trying to solve personal and relational problems (therapy, medications, spas, workshops, addictive behaviors).

3. Too many other people are involved with the problem—either irritated by it, worried about it, or trying to explain and solve it through overly serious means.

When any of these signs are present, it is likely that most of what you are doing about the situation is only making matters worse and that you are losing your spiritual arms, the horizontal pole of the shamanic cross. The attempted solutions are not helpful because the problem is being enlarged and concretized by too much seriousness. One's best source of hope in such a sinking and shrinking scenario is to jump headfirst into the Christian shaman's childlike world of uncommon sense, illogical experience, and sheer absurd mirth.

The lost directives that follow present you with some magical prescriptions that will help unwind and stretch out the world in which you are stuck. These undoings and unravelings can help bring forth the shamanic arms of the cross, enabling an opening of a spiritual door to new possibilities and deeper mysteries.

The lost directives are gifts from the ancestral spirits. They comprise a collection of shamanic tasks, strategies, and prescriptions for action that attempt to bring the winds and rains of mystical absurdity to arid, overly serious wastelands. The directives that follow are not meant simply to be read, nor are they meant as an amusement. Their purpose is to direct you to do something you may have never tried or imagined trying before. No matter how strange a directive may seem, do it! The power of shamanic action is not found in observing or thinking about it. The magic, enchantment, and wonder brought forth by Christian shamanism require one to loosen up one's over-seriousness—and that includes being too serious about Christianity!

In each of the chapters that follow, a message from spirit is first given as a shamanic teaching. It is followed by a collection of directives that aim to help you stretch your world and open you to new possibilities for shamanic transformation. The directives may be modified in any way that you desire. They are not rigid procedures, but are suggestions for how you can jump into life in a dramatically altered way. Feel free to tinker and improvise with them. I suggest a variety of "considerations" for each directive that helps you consider various ways of altering and thinking about them.

Should you find yourself wondering what is the point of an exercise, remind yourself that one of the points is to plunge you into a new experiential territory that bankrupts your habituated ways of making meaning. If you see "the point" of a particular directive, then consider modifying the exercise so you see no obvious point. This is intended to be a baptism into sacred absurdity, part of the matrix for shamanic transformation. You may want to find a shamanic buddy to be your partner in these exercises. This will empower the learning and make any performed nonsense more engaging and amusing.

With the lost directives and the lost teachings, both the horizontal and vertical poles of the cross emerge. The whole cross comprises a quaternary of outstretched opposites: creative imagination and spiritual truth (the vertical pole) crossed with serious suffering and absurd play (the horizontal pole). With the whole cross in play, the Christian shaman becomes an empowered participant in the ongoing dance of life and death.

# 15

# SHAMANIC DIRECTIVES
# fOR ADDRESSING WORRY

*For the foolishness of God is wiser than men, and the*
*weakness of God is stronger than men.*

1 CORINTHIANS 1:25

## SHAMANIC TEACHING

And so it was that the Lord intervened with wisdom that was dispersed
in the way of the sacred four. The sacred four became known as the four
directions, the four corners, the four edges of the sacred cross. The shamanic cross of the Christian shaman constitutes a whirl of never-ending
change. It is a cloud that blows itself from one corner to another. Around
the four corners, the spirit moves. Travel within the cross. Do not stop on
any corner, for to do so would be to spiritually die or hibernate until you
are awakened again. Move from one corner to another without cessation.
This is the way of the four-cornered shamanic cross.

The wolf of old came to teach. Without making a sound, the creature said:

*Know that the lost teachings that have been given to you—the*
*contemplations, meditations, lost parables, and active mystical*
*practices—are the seeds for shamanic vision and direct mystical*
*communion. They will carry you into deepened energetic expression*

*and heightened understanding. But this is not enough in itself. After receiving a deep understanding or being blessed with a vision from on high, you must not sit still and ponder. Immediately, you must jump into a sacred baptismal pool, an immersion into childlike madness, a retreat into absurd experience that washes away unnecessary attachment to the newfound wisdom. The teachings of spirit can be held only for a moment. If they are not immediately bathed in nonsense and frivolity, they begin to harden and turn into an opposite reality. They lose their innocent beauty and become hardened truths, truths whose brittleness cracks under the test of everyday movement and life. The wisdom of a contemplation, meditation, and parable can be preserved only by submerging it in the absurd. This is an ancient truth that no one is expected to fully understand.*

*Why, dear brothers and sisters, do the ancient traditions honor the trickster, fool, clown, and troublemaker? They surely know something we have forgotten. The outsiders who are seen as absurd from the perspective of consensual logical reality are necessary to maintain the bigger balance, the holding together of ancient wisdoms in the heart of everyday contradictions, temptations, challenges, and suffering. Bring the merriment and tomfoolery into your life or risk losing any lesson momentarily granted through visionary reflection and contemplative realization.*

*Know this and never forget it: The sufferings and shortcomings and difficulties and challenges of everyday life are necessary for things to work. They must be present in order for the shamanic realities to emerge. When worry comes your way, do not run from it. Do not fight it, numb yourself to its effects, or direct heroic efforts toward its elimination. Instead, embrace it as a presence you need to evolve your shamanic and spiritual nature. Reach out and hold onto worries and all other irritating disturbances. But while holding onto them, proceed to play and alter your worries. Juxtapose their troubling presence with an altered presence that makes them child's play. When the serious and ridiculous are juxtaposed and stretched, the portals to spiritual knowledge are opened.*

As you practice the forgotten directives presented below, know they are not intended to alleviate your problems and worries. You can't stop worrying. That is a given. But you can match the seriousness and despair of your worries with an oppositional force that plays with them. Yes, you will continue to worry and wake up in the middle of the night wondering how to solve your dilemmas. But now you can meet that serious worrying with some playful worrying. Playing with your worries in a shamanic way creates a shamanic dichotomy in your life. Now you are stretched between two poles: the pole of serious worrying and the pole of playful, frivolous worrying. As these two poles are stretched further and further, you make possible a new energy in your life, a creative tension that can break open an entry into the great mysteries.

## ✦ DIRECTIVE: THE BOUNCING BALL

Obtain the tiniest rubber ball you can find and carry it with you. Whenever you catch yourself worrying, throw this ball in the air and pretend you're going to catch it. Then purposefully miss catching the ball and let it hit the ground. Immediately say quietly to yourself, "You've got to fall all the way to the ground in order to rise again. In this way, the cross is stretched further and further." Repeat this procedure every time you catch yourself worrying.

### Considerations
- What color ball will you choose?
- Will you draw a mystical symbol on it?
- How high will you throw it? Will it depend on how worried you are?
- Can you learn to look forward to not catching the ball?
- Make this your mantra: *You must fall in order to rise. In this way the cross is stretched further and further.* Write it down. Write it again with a different color of ink. Sing it.
- Is there a place you should go to practice this directive?
- Consider making a prayer for this practice.
- Will you obtain different balls for different kinds of concerns and worries?

- Consider having a different ball for each month of the year.
- Will you find a special place in your home where your ball can rest?
- What can you do to honor your special ball?

## ✦ DIRECTIVE: THE WORRY-FREE COINS

Make a list of three things that you can't possibly imagine yourself worrying about. For each worry-free item, select a color. For instance, you might come up with something like this:

1. Opening a book that you are not interested in reading: Blue
2. Washing a sidewalk: Green
3. Reading a phone book: White

When you have made your list and color assignments, select three dimes. With a marking pen, color each dime. Make certain to color both sides of the coins with the colors you selected earlier.

Carry these worriless coins in your pocket or purse. Whenever you start to really worry about something, pull out all three coins and shake them in your hand. Let them fall from your hand onto a table surface. Carefully note which ones fall as "heads" and which as "tails." If there are any heads, place them on top of your own head for five seconds. For any coins that land as tails, pick them up and spank them with one of your little fingers. If you don't get a head, then repeat the procedure until you do get one. After the heads have been placed on your head and the tails have been spanked, place the coins back into your pocket. Say quietly to yourself, "It is important to stretch my foolishness. May the arms of the cross come forth."

### Considerations
- Can you worry about what you worry about?
- If you worry more about worriless things, might you worry less about other things?
- Consider how shaking the coins could influence the effectiveness of this directive.

- Experiment with vigorous versus gentle shaking methods.
- How many different ways of spanking your tails can you come up with?
- Could you have chosen other colors for your coins? Is color important?
- Consider whether practicing absurd directives in a serious fashion helps you become a holy fool.

## ✦ DIRECTIVE: CHALK MAGIC

Obtain a magnifying glass and a tiny chalkboard. Before retiring one night, plan to wake up ten minutes earlier than usual the next morning. When you awaken, get up, go to your chalkboard, and write down what you are most spiritually worried about. If you aren't sure, just write down your best guess. For the next five minutes, focus all your attention upon examining what you wrote. Do this by looking at it through a magnifying glass. You are not to look at your worry without magnification. When you are finished looking, wipe the board clean with your fingers. Open your Bible and rub the chalk along the page that is opened. You can decide for yourself whether you will read the page that has been whitened. Repeat this procedure every morning for two weeks. After that time, limit studying your worries to three mornings a week.

## Considerations

- Consider how the meaning of anything is shaped by the magnification through which it is observed.
- Consider getting different kinds of magnifying glasses with different strengths.
- After you have rubbed the chalk along your Bible page, wipe a bit of it over your third eye (the place on your forehead between and just above your eyes). Do this before reading the scripture. Consider it a magnifying light for spiritual understanding.
- Use the chalk on your Bible page as a spiritual medicine. Wipe some over your heart before going to sleep, asking for a spiritual

dream to touch your heart. Consider it a lighthouse for the spirit to find.

- Experiment with different colors of chalk.
- Try to guess what you are worried about on a deep, unconscious level, below your conscious awareness.
- Write down some worries that really aren't worries. Pretend they are big worries.
- Write down the word "worry" in three different sizes. Make that your list of worries.
- Make up nonsense sentences and words for your list of worries. Might they provide clues for inner spiritual work? If any word seems to stand out in an unusual way, consider it a clue. Think about that word throughout the next day or two and see whether it inspires a useful insight.

### ✦ DIRECTIVE: SHAKING THE RUG

Obtain a small rug that you can roll up and hide in a place that will remain undisturbed by others. When you find yourself worrying too much, pull out the rug and place it on the floor. Take off your shoes and socks and stand on the rug while holding a cross.

While standing, tap your head with the cross and imagine all of your worries traveling from your head to your feet. Ask your mind to let go of holding the worries in your head. Allow gravity and the tapping of your cross to drop those worries to the bottom of your feet.

As your worries begin moving toward your feet, wiggle your toes, pretending that this is caused by the worries entering the lowest place on your body. Wiggle them for at least ten seconds and then stomp and move your feet on the mat so that you completely shake out those worries. When the worries are out, close your eyes and imagine that your body has grown taller. Imagine this as a stretching of the vertical pole of your internal cross. When you have vigorously completed this task, pick up the rug, take it outside, and shake it so your worries won't stick to your rug. Roll up the rug and give it a rest so it will be ready the next time you need to use it.

## Considerations

- Consider using different sizes and kinds of crosses. Empower your cross by a ritual that you create. Perhaps you will sing it a sacred song, immerse it in holy water, or paint it, among other possibilities.
- Experiment with different kinds of rugs.
- Consider how many times you will tap your head with the cross. Should it be a magical number?
- Rather than stomping your feet, try dancing in a spirited way. Make sure, however, that your feet hit the ground with a pronounced impact.
- Try doing this with a partner. Be together on the rug and with the dance.
- Add some music or drumming to the background.
- Consider what direction you should face when you tap the cross on your head.

## ✦ DIRECTIVE: THE ANGEL'S PIGGY BANK

Make your own piggy bank out of a jar or box. Attach cardboard wings to its sides and call it the angel's piggy bank. Place it on top of your television.

Every time you find yourself worrying for longer than a minute, place a quarter into that bank. You must be honest and feed the bank whenever you worry too much.

When the bank is full, donate the money to a worthy spiritual organization that works with children. Tell yourself that you can now stop worrying about your worrying because you have put that worrying to work. Your worrying now helps others, even when you're unable to help yourself. Continue this practice for as long as you feel it is providing a teaching.

## Considerations

- Consider raising the stakes. Raise the amount donated to one dollar rather than a quarter.

- Spend at least ten minutes a day worrying about what organization deserves your donation.
- Find someone else who will do this with you. Make it a competition over who can give away the most money. Award the winner each month, perhaps by taking them to dinner.
- Ponder the guilt or unease you may experience if you begin to enjoy giving away charitable gifts while getting tired of worrying. Start preparing for worries that you feel better about, such as raising money to help others.
- As there is a change in the pattern of your worries or worrying, begin planning to replace the bank with a new pair of wings.

## ✦ DIRECTIVE: WORRY-OF-THE-MONTH CLUB

Go to a print shop and have some stationery made for you with these words printed on it:

WORRY-OF-THE-
MONTH CLUB

On the first day of each month, select a worry you will focus on. Using your stationery, write yourself this letter:

Dear Worrier,

    This month's worry is_____. You are to pledge that no matter how many worries you have or however much worrying you take on, this worry is to be worried about the most.

Sincerest worrying,
President, Worry-of-the-Month Club

Write and mail this letter to yourself every other day throughout the month. When you receive the letter, say the Lord's Prayer before opening it, but make sure that you leave one or two words out of the prayer. Worry about which words to drop.

## Considerations

- Consider making an oversized business card for your Worry-of-the-Month Club.
- Print your card in a foreign language.
- Keep a record of the words you drop out of the Lord's Prayer. Explore the possible unconscious motivations behind your choices.
- Change the Lord's Prayer to another prayer.

## ✦ DIRECTIVE: WORRY SWAPPING

Find another spiritually inspired person who worries as much as you do. For one week, swap your worries. Each person must make a list of his or her top worries and give it to the other. Be sincere in your efforts to worry daily about the other's worries. Always say, "God bless these worries" before you start worrying. You may find that learning to worry about the other person's concerns helps you put your own worries in a different perspective, thereby making you a better servant of God's will.

## Considerations

- Are there different ways to pretend worrying? For example, do you pretend to be the other person or do you simply pretend to have their worries? Can you pretend to be God (or a helping angel) worrying about both of you? Consider other ways of pretending to worry.
- Maybe you would prefer to say, "In the name of the Holy One, please anoint these worries" before you start worrying.
- When you make your bedtime prayer, add a sentence that says, "And please watch over my worries and help them teach me to be a better servant of thy will."

- On the first day of worrying for someone else's worries, welcome them into your home. You might get them a welcome present that is appropriately wrapped, or bake a special cake and hold a party.
- You could keep the list of the other person's worries in the guest room or on the guest bed.

## ✦ DIRECTIVE: GOD'S WORRIES

Have three people who know you well write down what they think God should worry about, if God were to worry. They are not to show or tell you what worries they choose for you. For a week you are to worry about whether or not you can guess the worries they selected. At the end of the week, they are to tell you what worries they chose for you so you can find out whether you did a good job. If you guessed most of the worries correctly, spend the evening worrying about how you should celebrate your victory. If you guessed most of them incorrectly, then spend the evening worrying about how to do the exercise over again for a more successful outcome, entitling you to worry about a future victory celebration.

### Considerations

- What worries might an evil entity such as Satan select for you?
- How are God's worries and Satan's worries different? Are they really that different?
- If you guess the worries correctly, does that mean that you really know the other person—or would it be more accurate to say that the other person really knows you?
- What worries might God select for Satan? Make sure they are worries that would constitute good teaching.
- What worries would Satan select for God to make God a better supreme being?
- Are you a good enough worrier to assist God in your afterlife? Do you qualify to be a "worry angel" who gives people healthy worries? If not, what must you learn or change to become qualified for that position?

## ✦ DIRECTIVE: THE MAGIC RING

Get yourself a small box, the kind of box jewelry stores use for gift wrapping merchandise. Make certain it has a soft piece of cotton in it. Decorate the outside of the box with religious symbols that have meaning for you. After you have set up this box, spend some time looking for and purchasing a toy ring.

Place the ring on the middle of your forehead and pretend to send all of the worries in your mind into it. Go through some improvised shamanic motions to make that ring vibrate on your forehead. After you have done this, carefully center the ring in the small box. Allow the ring to spend the night in the box. The next day, take the ring out and wrap the empty box in some interesting wrapping paper. Attach the ring to the outside of the box as if it were a decorative part of the gift wrapping.

Contact a friend or relative and ask them to do you a favor. Tell them you are worried about mishandling an important spiritual gift you've recently wrapped. Ask if they will keep the gift for you for the next two weeks. Don't tell them what it is. If they ask, say it's a shamanic surprise and you can't tell anyone.

After two weeks, ask your friend to give back the gift. Take your friend to lunch and bring the gift with you. After you've eaten lunch, tell your friend the gift was a spiritual gift for yourself. Explain that you knew you wouldn't be able to keep from meddling with it unless someone else kept it for you. Thank your friend for helping you and go home with the unopened gift. If they ask what's inside the box, simply say, "Oh, I can't say, but it's really nothing. It's a kind of Zen gift for shamans." Never unwrap the box.

### Considerations

- What if you had purchased an expensive ring? Would that make any difference in how you felt about the exercise? Contemplate the difference it might have made to put the ring inside the box, instead of on the outside. Does it matter if our treasures are on the inside or the outside, seen or hidden?

- Are there other ways of wrapping the present or using other symbols that would more effectively arouse your friend's curiosity?
- Where might you put your gift after you finish this directive? Bury it under a tree? Place it in the back of a dresser drawer? Mail it to yourself on a monthly basis?

## ✦ DIRECTIVE: BIG AND IMPORTANT SPIRITUAL WORRIES

Ask everyone you know to list the three most important spiritual issues every person on the planet should worry about. Write down these responses in a notebook. Conduct this research in a very determined way. Do your best to find out what others believe should be the BIG AND IMPORTANT SPIRITUAL WORRIES.

When you believe you have identified these big and important spiritual worries, write the following letter:

To Whom It May Concern:

    I am a concerned citizen who on my own began asking as many people as I could the following question: "What are the three most important spiritual concerns everyone on the planet should worry about?"

    Based on this research, I found that most people believe we should be spiritually worried about:

1. _____
2. _____
3. _____

    As someone who cares and worries about the future, I sincerely ask you to do some thoughtful worrying about these three spiritual issues. I can assure you that I will be doing my own worrying. Will you please consider doing your part?

Most sincerely,
A World Worrier

Make copies of this letter and place it everywhere you possibly can. Give some thought to what it would be like to devote your life to a project of serious spiritual worrying.

One month after leaving as many of these letters as you can around your community, turn to the appendix "Message for the World Worrier" and read the message as a consideration of your work (try not to read it until that time).

## CONCLUDING THOUGHTS

The Christian shaman knows that everyone will worry. What matters is whether you are engaged in unhealthy worrying or resourceful worrying. Unhealthy worrying is psychological quicksand—the more you worry, the more worried you get. The problem doesn't get resolved, but escalates in its intensity. In the beginning of your encounter with any particular worry, it is wise to pray for help, asking God to take over your worries. That's always a good thing to do. However, if you keep praying to God for help, it may send the message that you don't think God is listening or that you doubt whether God can help. Pray once with sincerity and then let it go. After that, prayer isn't needed.

After the prayer has been made, it's time to bring levity and shamanic play into the picture. With this posture you trust that God will take care of things and that there is nothing left to do on the serious side of things. Now it's time to give the trickster part of you its due. Meet the arrival of worry with strategies of absurdity. The directives in this chapter have shown you ways in which you can experiment, tinker, improvise, and play with your worries. They show how worry can be the existential core for you to process and refine into nuggets of learning, teaching you how to be a trickster shaman. We will continue looking at how other daily nuisances and problems can be similarly utilized so as to help you stretch the arms of the Christian shaman's cross.

# 16

# SHAMANIC DIRECTIVES
# FOR ADDRESSING
# SELF-IMAGE

*For as he thinketh in his heart, so is he.*

PROVERBS 23:7

## SHAMANIC TEACHING

How does the Christian shaman regard the importance of self? The Master taught that only those who lose themselves may find themselves. Paradox rules the shamanic world. Opposites tease out truth through the push and pull of contrary ideas: One must existentially die in order to resurrect a new life. Lose your importance to find out what is important. Laugh to find the truth of tears, and cry to find the truth of laughter. The Christian shaman cannot escape the riddles, mirages, delusions, reversed truths, paradoxes, polyrhythms, and polyphonies of self. In this vein, self-image must include a noncaring and even a ridiculing of how we and others see us. Herein lies the escape from the suffering related to issues about self-image.

One shamanic mission in everyday life is to counter our serious considerations of self (including its surrender) with frivolous play. We must play with all of our notions of self and self-image in order to create a shamanic dichotomy that pushes and pulls us toward mystical knowing.

In the shamanic dialectic lies the possibility for mystical emergence. The old ones talk about these things:

> *Pay no excessive attention to your concern for self and self-image. Likewise, devote no excessive concern to the elimination of concern for your image. Let each thought of self pass by like dust in the wind. Try to meet serious concern for self with the shamanic antidote of absurd play. Play brings about a tension that creates energy and the possibility of spiritual transformation.*
>
>   *Embrace your obsessions and reduce them to absurdity. See yourself through trickster eyes. Do so endlessly, until play overcomes any steady concern or particular self-image. Change your image and change it again. Receive these forms without judgment, allowing them to pass with all other thoughts. As images emerge, send them to the playing field. There creation will continue, shifting, changing for all time.*

As we played with worry, now shall we play with concerns for self-image. The old ones say that it is not enough to have direct mystical communion. The realization of the divine will shake your whole being, setting forth vibrations that can level mountains. And this can open the gate to visions that inspire new ways of living. However, this in itself is not enough either. Vision left alone turns stale and seduces one into believing it is a hard and fast truth. When taken too literally, the deepest and highest truths shrink and evaporate. Visionary truth must be leveled to the ground and held there by outstretched spiritual arms, a task best accomplished with quaking laughter and merry play. Then the truth will be protected from the concretizing forces of certainty and judgment. Truth, to remain truth, must be kept hidden, obscured and invisible. Any truth that can still be seen is a fading truth, and when permanently brought into view, it will inevitably become a lie.

Take yourself seriously only as long as it takes you to notice that you are taking yourself seriously. Then play with your image, your identity, and your belief about who and what you are. Allow your play to erode any and all fixed knowing. Stand under your understanding and throw it in the air, juggling it without end. In this way, you will stay innocent and ignorant as a child, full of wonder and empty of settled knowledge.

In this emptiness dwells the four-cornered cross, representing movement from serious realization and momentary vision to creative inspiration and expression, to absurd baptism that purifies, readying you for the next lightning bolt of life to startle and surprise you, causing every bone in your body to shake and rattle. In this movement from one corner of the cross to another, the four corners make a temple for the holy of holies.

Prepare to face your image and accept the inevitable fact that you cannot help being interested in who and what you are. Invite the jester that resides within. Destroy your momentary selves with merciless teasing and play. Fully consider the shamanic axiom, "To know yourself, change!" Allow the winds of absurdity to blow.

## ✦ DIRECTIVE: SELF STEAM

Make a list of everything you can describe or say about your "self." This list should be as complete and exhaustive as you can make it. Make sure that you emphasize your shamanic qualities. Work on this list for at least a week. You may spend longer than that if necessary.

When the list is complete, take a sharp pair of scissors and cut the descriptions of your self into as many tiny pieces as you can. Place these tiny pieces into a pot of water. Now place this pot over some heat and boil the mixture. When the steam begins to rise, carefully look at the steam and say aloud, "This is the steam arising from everything I know about my self. It is my self steam." Go on to make this simple prayer: "Lord, I ask that you turn my eyes away from my *self-esteem* and direct them to the holy ghost mist of your presence."

### Considerations

- Pay attention to how often people talk about self-esteem.
- When you hear someone say self-esteem, translate it to yourself as *spiritual steam*.

- Consider moving away from the psychology of self-esteem to the spirituality of holy steam.
- Repeat the directive, but this time boil your descriptions in water seasoned with salt. While doing this, reflect upon the biblical story of Lot's wife turning around to recall her luxurious life in Sodom and being turned into a pillar of salt.
- When you notice you have moved away from self-esteem and toward spiritual steam, ask yourself whether you will consider eating less salt with some of your meals.

## ✦ DIRECTIVE: THE BAPTIZED SPOT

Carefully examine your whole body. Identify a particular spot no larger than a circle with a one-inch diameter. This spot should be intriguing for you to look at. It should feel spiritually important. There is no need to know why it feels that way. It should only feel like an important spiritual place on your body. It may be anywhere on your body—the bottom of your foot, the palm of your hand, your earlobe, eye, or kneecap. Feel free to use a mirror. When you have chosen your spot, spend five minutes each day observing it. Come to know it well, becoming aware of its many details and special features. After a week of doing this, see if you know it well enough to see it in your mind. You may make a drawing if you wish.

When the spot is clearly a part of your consciousness, give it a biblical name. You may have to consult the Bible to help you make the choice. For three days, refer to this part of your body by its new name. Keep doing this until it no longer feels strange to say the name.

As soon as you notice that you are feeling comfortable calling your spot by its new name, write down the time and date at which this transformation took place. For some people, it may only take several days. For others, it may take months. However long it takes, on the day you make the transition to familiarity, record the time it happened. After you have recorded this information, immediately fill a glass of water, hold it over the Bible for a moment, and then pour it over the spot on your body. Consider this act a special baptism.

## Considerations

- Consider repeating this directive until you have baptized every spot on your body.
- Imagine baptizing your spot with other liquids—sparkling water, wine, fruit juice, olive oil, river water, and so forth.
- If you continued and baptized other spots, how many names would you need?
- Give your whole body the name of a village mentioned in the Bible and consider the baptized spots its residents.
- What if your ceremony for blessing the water took several hours? Would that make the baptism more meaningful?
- If you were to baptize many spots, which would be the holiest and most honored spot?

## ✦ DIRECTIVE: YOUR HOLY LAND

Obtain an illustration of Jesus. Once you have the image, immediately get a map of the city or town where you live. With a pair of scissors, carefully cut your sacred image of Jesus into at least four pieces. Glue or tape the top piece of the image of Jesus to the corresponding northern portion of the map. Do the same for the other pieces of your image, making sure each piece is located in the correct geographical location on the map. You should end up with a map of your geographical area that has pieces of the image of Jesus attached in all four directions.

Go to one of the areas on the map to which a piece of your image is attached. When you arrive at this location, cut out the appropriate piece of the map with the sacred image on it. Bury it in the ground at that location. Go throughout the city or town, doing this for every piece of your image of Jesus.

After you have completed the task, practice the following contemplation twice daily. Before you fall asleep and immediately upon awakening, devote one minute to seeing in your mind's eye the pieces of the image of Jesus spread all over the region in which you live. Briefly consider how your self-image can change when seen resting inside the image of Jesus.

## Considerations

- Reflect on how this directive creates a secret holy land out of the area in which you live.
- Consider doing the same thing with other sacred images, whether from Christianity (using Mary and the saints) or other world religions.
- Think of the spiritual needs of your holy land. Do the pieces of the image(s) need to be given offerings? Should you conduct a monthly or annual ceremony in which you visit a particular site or sites?
- What if you made a treasure map that enabled someone to find the pieces of the divine image? Where would you leave the map?
- Give your holy land a sacred name. Consider this the new address for your self-image.

## ✦ Directive: Spiritually Seasoning Your Life Stories

Lie down on a large piece of white paper and have someone trace the outline of your body. On this true-to-scale outline of yourself, do the following:

1. With colored pencils representing your favorite colors, slowly and patiently color it in. Make certain you fill in the whole image with color.
2. Go to your family members, friends, and colleagues, inviting them to sign your body image. Pull out the specially prepared paper and instruct them to write down their favorite memory about something the two of you did together. Make certain that they sign their name next to the memory. If they ask why you are doing this, you may say that it is a shamanic assignment.
3. You should fill up the remaining space with five Bible verses. You may repeat the verses as often as is required to fill the space. Make sure that every scripture has special significance to you.
4. When the body image is full of memories and biblical wisdom, place it under your bed. It should be aligned in such a way that it lines up with where you sleep.

5. Throughout each day, wonder about whether you will dream about the image that lies underneath your bed. Remind yourself that it has been "seasoned" with the holy word. Ask God to spiritually bake this preparation, as if it were a dish going into an oven, and serve it to you as a special dream.

## Considerations

- Consider folding up your image and making it into a small bundle. Go a step further and surround it with clay. Place it underneath your bed and go to bed wondering whether you are being remolded.
- If you don't want to ask other people to write their favorite memories, consider inventing memories for famous people. Write these down and sign the fantasized person's name.
- Consider sprinkling your favorite spices onto the image. Will they be sweet, sour, or spicy?
- Perhaps you could change the seasoning every night, depending upon your mood. The image could be heavily peppered one night, followed by a sprinkling of basil the next evening.
- In the morning, put on some potholders and remove the image, behaving as if you are pulling it out of the oven.

## ✦ DIRECTIVE: THE BUTTON

Take twelve close-up photographs of your belly button. After they are developed, write zany Christian shamanic captions under each photograph, for instance, "Ezekiel's Crater," "Jacob's Bull's Eye," "Do Not Touch This Button Unless It Is a Spiritual Emergency," "Journey to the Center of Jerusalem," "Lint Temple," and so forth. Do not label more than one photograph per day. Place these photographs in a scrapbook that is clearly titled, *Meditations on My Center: Beginnings of Christian Shamanism.*

## Considerations

- Rather than placing the photographs in a scrapbook, place them inside your Bible.

- Add a biblical scripture to each zany caption. Choose them at random. Consider the juxtaposition of the caption and the scripture as a spiritual dissonance that jazzes up your shamanic life.
- Consider painting your belly button or drawing symbols on or around it before you photograph it.
- Think about placing a button on your belly button.
- Lie down and pour some planting soil on your belly button. Place a small cross in it and sprinkle a bit of water over the soil. Stay in this position for one hour while imagining that you are growing a new understanding of your spiritual life.

## ✦ DIRECTIVE: DREAM HALO

Ask a child, either your own child or the child of a friend or relative, to draw a picture of you with a halo over your head. Provide the child with crayons or watercolors if he or she needs them. What is absolutely critical is that you never see the picture. When it is finished, ask someone to place it in an envelope and seal it.

Take this hidden image of yourself with a halo and insert it into the middle of your pillow. You may have to take your pillow to someone with sewing skills and have them open your pillow, place the envelope in it, and then sew it up. From time to time throughout the weeks that follow, arrange to take a few minutes to rest your head upon this pillow and contemplate how the child may have seen you. Use this pillow for sleeping through the night no more than once every three days.

### Considerations
- Draw a picture of yourself as you think the child may have drawn it and ask the child if it is similar. You get three tries.
- Draw a halo on the bottom of each of your feet before you go to sleep. Think about how you are haloed from head to toe.
- Consider getting a pillowcase in the color that you believe is your most important spiritual color.
- If you have a dream while sleeping on the special pillow, write it down on the pillowcase.

- If you don't have a dream after sleeping on the special pillow, make up a dream and pretend to write it on the pillowcase.

## ✦ DIRECTIVE: MULTIPLE IMAGES

Go through some spiritual magazines and books and identify photographs or drawings of spiritual leaders and teachers who have qualities you desire. Proceed to make a copy or cut them out. You should have at least twenty-five images. For the next week, spend some time every day looking at these images and becoming familiar with them.

The following week, spend the same amount of time examining them. This time, however, you are to pretend they are photographs (or drawings) of you in disguise. Stare at each image while pretending that a Hollywood makeup artist transformed you into looking like the picture you see.

On the third week, glue all of the pictures together so that the whole stack is one solid whole. On top of this pile glue photographs of yourself that you think don't really look like you. You may have to actually create disguises and have new photographs taken.

Place this amalgam of images under the chair in your home in which you sit most frequently. Try to never think of it again.

### Considerations
- Consider choosing images of "crazy wisdom" teachers, fools, and tricksters.
- Photograph yourself looking as zany or absurd as possible and include this picture with the pictures of the spiritual teachers.
- Think of unexpected places your images could be placed—over the shower, in the refrigerator, inside your Bible. This time, rather than trying to ignore the images, pay close attention to them.
- Choose one image that you like best and actually ask a makeup artist to help make you look like that person for a day.

## ✦ DIRECTIVE: THE BOOK OF SIGNINGS

Purchase a book of blank pages. On each page sign a biblical name. Do not sign this name in a hurry. Take your time and do it carefully. Do not use the same pen more than once. Each signature requires a different pen. Borrow these pens from people you know. You may have to walk around with your book and from time to time ask a friend if you may borrow their pen. In this way you can collect one signature at a time.

When the book of signatures is complete, wrap it up in a package and mail it to yourself. When it is delivered to you, unwrap the package, sit down with the book, and carefully read every page.

Repeat this process three times—wrapping, mailing, and reading. After the third reading, type the instructions you have followed from this book. Attach these instructions to the inside of your signature book.

Arrange to take a trip to a town you have never visited. Go to the public library and leave your book of biblical signatures on a shelf with other books. Make certain you haven't forgotten to include the instructions for making the book. Before you depart, write one question in the book, doing so on the last page: "Do these names live in your heart?"

### Considerations

- Consider choosing your favorite biblical name, a name that you like better than your own, or a name that you like as much as your own, or one that you don't like at all, and make this the title of the book.
- Write some of the signatures while holding onto a certain feeling or attitude. Some of the signatures might be written while you are relaxed, while other signings should be done when you are feeling (or pretending to feel) stress, anger, jealousy, peace, love, hate, irritation, tenderness, and so forth.
- In what section of the library will you leave the signings? Might it be biography, history, religion, self-help, humor, philosophy, cooking, sports, or language?
- Consider adding another sentence to the last page: "Do we spend enough time thinking about these spirit guides?"
- Designate a page for signing with invisible ink, real or imaginary.

## ✦ DIRECTIVE: MAGNIFYING MAGNIFICENCE

Purchase a paint kit and use it once for this specific task. Paint the ugliest picture you are capable of producing. You may throw paint on the paper or canvas, stomp on it, scratch it, or do whatever it takes to make it as ugly and as offensive as possible. When the picture is complete, throw away the paint and brush.

Sit down with the painting and examine it with a magnifying glass. Try not to look at the whole picture. Observe it only through the magnifying glass. Under this different level of magnification, find a piece of the picture that appears beautiful and interesting to you.

Cut out this tiny piece of the picture that appears beautiful when observed with magnification. Dispose of the rest of the picture and only keep the little piece you cut out. Mount this piece onto a backboard or surface that can be placed into a picture frame. Purchase a magnificent frame for your work of art and place it on the desk or area where you spend most of your time working.

From now on, keep this secret to yourself:

*Ugliness and beauty are the same. Any difference between the two can be attributed to magnification. Magnificence is created by magnification. God's view is always that of magnification and magnificence.*

### Considerations

- When you see something you don't like in the world, quietly ask yourself, "How much does it need to be magnified before I can see its beauty?"
- Spend five minutes a day meditating on the idea that some large things appear ugly, but when reduced in size, they look beautiful.
- Carry a tiny magnifying glass with you. When you find yourself disturbed by an ugly situation, including things people say, hold onto your magnifying glass.
- Remember that beautiful things may also appear ugly when seen through different magnification.

- Write the word "ugly" on one side of a magnifying glass and the word "beautiful" on the other side. Place the glass underneath your Bible and say, "Even the Bible can be seen as beautiful or ugly. The difference depends on the magnification."
- Hold a magnifying glass in front of you and imagine that an invisible person is looking at you through it. Does your self-image change when you imagine the invisible observer's magnified view?

## ✦ DIRECTIVE: TAMING A COIN

Go to a coin shop and purchase an old coin that appears exotic or mysterious to you. Its economic value is not important. What matters is that you are drawn to the coin in some way.

During the first week after purchasing and bringing this coin home, you are to make it a member of your household. On its first night home, allow it to sit only in your favorite chair. When you retire for the evening, take it to bed with you. Allow it to sleep near your pillow. Mention it in your prayers. Bring it with you to every meal and place it next to your plate. Throughout the day, hold the coin many times in each hand. From time to time you might even drop it inside your shoe when you sit down to take a rest. Try doing as many things as you can think of to become acquainted with your coin and to make it feel like it belongs with you.

After a week of "shamanically taming" your coin, take or find a photograph of yourself in which the size of your head would just cover one side of the coin. Cut out your head and permanently glue it to one side of the coin. Being as serious as you can, have someone take a photograph of your posterior. (It may be appropriate for you to keep it clothed.) Using a photocopier if necessary to shrink the photograph, create an image of your posterior that will fit on the other side of the coin. Permanently glue this cut-out shot of your backside to the coin.

You are never to show this coin to anyone. Find a secret place where the coin can be held. Perhaps you can keep it inside the pages of a book in the Bible that others seldom read.

When you find yourself filled with doubts about yourself or any aspect of your being, do the following procedure. Get out your special coin and flip it in the air saying, "For many people life is just a matter of heads and tails. They often choose decisions, attitudes, and understandings by the flip of a coin." Then look at both sides of your coin and ask yourself aloud, "Do I really want to determine the course of my life based on the difference between a head and a tail?" If and only if you catch yourself smiling or laughing, you may open a spiritual book that evening and permit yourself to read a random paragraph.

## Considerations

- How many people do you know who would enjoy hearing about this spiritual exercise?
- How many people do you know who would do it?
- Find more people in your life that would do this kind of practice.
- Consider this an evangelical mission for shamanic Christianity.
- Make up a story of how doing this practice changed your life. Pretend that it brought about an "absurd conversion," making you more respectful of being odd in a kind, playful, and harmless way.

### ✦ DIRECTIVE: WALKING THE CROSS

Make certain you have a collection of colored marking pens available. When you wake up tomorrow morning, decide which color you like the best and which you like the least. Take the pens that indicate your two color choices and make a small cross on the bottom of the heel of each foot. On each foot, make each line of the cross a different one of the two colors.

Throughout the day, catch yourself whenever you find yourself feeling concerned about how you look to others. When you catch yourself, stomp your feet and grind your heels into the floor or ground. Think about how there are two intersecting lines on each heel. One line represents a color you dislike and the other line represents a color you like. Realize that no one else knows about or sees these two crossed lines. No one else knows that you are standing on top of the difference between what you like and dislike.

Make certain you examine your heels at the end of the day. Wash away the colored lines and be prepared to do this every other day for two weeks. Do not try to think about any connections between the cross and what it has to do with the burden you carry about your self-image.

### Considerations

- Try using different color combinations. Try a line of dots rather than a continuous line.
- Consider making a cross of one color for the left foot and another color for the right foot.
- What if you make a circle within a circle, rather than two intersecting lines?
- Examine each heel at the bottom of the day. Say in private, "This is the result of life meeting the cross. A new, revitalized cross must be made for each day."
- Would you ever tattoo a cross on the bottom of each heel?

## CONCLUDING THOUGHTS

I propose that a commitment to these shamanic directives is more likely to transform your self-image than any time spent in psychotherapy or in drug-induced altered states of consciousness. As strange as some of the practices may seem, performing them with a strong intent to transform yourself is one of the most powerful things you can do. It's that simple: Radically alter your daily conduct and the world around you will reorganize itself. For example, carrying a mirror with you that has the photograph of a galaxy taped to it can change your life. If you pick up the mirror at least a dozen times a day and pretend that you are looking at your image, your unconscious will be fed a steady diet of messages that say, "You are the universe." Over time, this will sink in and change how you perceive your presence in the cosmos.

Similarly, all the directives in this chapter have played with any concern you may have about your image. Whether baptizing parts of your body, discovering your self steam, or changing your level of magnification, these shamanic exercises disrupt the seldom examined premises about who you think you are. These immersions into absurdity loosen the tightly held negative assumptions about yourself that hold you back from meeting all of your inborn potential. In the loosening, other possibilities become present and the seeds for significant transformation are planted.

# 17

# SHAMANIC DIRECTIVES
# FOR ADDRESSING
# MOTIVATION

*And my speech and my preaching were not in persuasive*
*words of wisdom, but in demonstration of the Spirit and*
*of Power: that your faith should not stand in the wisdom*
*of men, but in the power of God.*

1 CORINTHIANS 2:1–5

## SHAMANIC TEACHING

To God be the glory for those times in which inspiration flows. The days and nights fly by, infused with a motivation that is effortless, unlearned, and unearned. It is simply there, powering us to fly through our life. And then it stops, and we are left stranded on an island of immobility. How do we get inspired and motivated to move again? This dilemma visits us throughout our lives. It is part of the ebb and flow of everyday living. The presence and absence of motivation is a breath that goes in and out with its own natural cycles.

When motivation becomes an issue, we may worry, fret, and concern ourselves with recharging our inspirational batteries. When the absence of motivation is upon us, we try to pick ourselves up and get remotivated. The shaman who understands the four-cornered cross knows that something can be done—and undone—when we are left stranded with no desire to live fully. Shamans recognize that motivation runs dry in the absence of creative expression and absurd merriment. When one is caught in motivational depravity, it is time to call for an infusion of playful absurdity. This, in turn, gives rise to creative impulses and the subsequent flow of the life force.

Enter into the dried motivation spells and counter them with an incantation of absurd play. Allow the voice of unreason to quiet the overly trained problem-solving mind. Think of your rational intelligence and your emotional intelligence. Now consider your nonsense intelligence. Give it some playtime. Allow it to sweep away the cobwebs that prevent you from seeing rays of hope and newfound inspiration. Allow yourself to plunge into the absurd.

## ✦ DIRECTIVE: SHAMANIC MOTIVATION STRIPS

The next time you find yourself thinking, "I wish I had more motivation," do the following. With scissors cut out twenty-five strips of paper. On each piece of paper write the words SHAMANIC MOTIVATION in capital letters.

Obtain a medium-sized glass jar. Place your strips of shamanic motivation into this jar. Do this every time you worry whether or not you have enough motivation. When the jar becomes full of shamanic motivation strips, you can proceed to the next step.

The first time you catch yourself being motivated to pray and actually do it, take one shamanic motivation strip out of your big jar. Write down what you prayed about on the back side of the strip of paper. Place this strip inside a brand-new Bible you have never opened before. Continue filling this Bible with your descriptions of truly motivated prayer.

When you have fed your Bible all the strips, find a spiritually oriented person who is having a motivational problem and share this procedure with him or her. Make them promise that they, too, will pass on the knowledge to someone else when they finish making their motivated Bible.

## *Considerations*

- What difference might it make if you cut out strips of cloth instead of paper and hung them over your Bible instead of placing them inside its pages?
- Do any of the motivational strips seem stronger to you than others? Consider coloring these with colors you like and placing them in your Bible, perhaps on a page with a favorite passage.
- Rather than place the strips inside your Bible, imagine taping them to the outside of the Bible.
- After the strips have lived in your Bible for a while, consider taking them to your yard or someplace in the woods and burying them near a tree.
- Rather than bury your strips, ponder attaching them to helium balloons and releasing them into the atmosphere.

## ✦ DIRECTIVE: THE LITTLE ENGINE THAT COULD

Purchase three different-sized beach balls so you have a small, medium, and large one. On each ball write the words, "I think I can. I think I can." The next time you worry about your motivation, determine whether it is a small, medium, or large motivational problem. Choose the beach ball that fits the size of your problem.

Now blow up the beach ball in this special way: After each puff of air, say, "I think I can. I think I can." Make certain that you do this in the presence of two things: a lit candle and the classic children's book, *The Little Engine That Could*. Keep your three balls, a candle, and the book together and never do this procedure unless the candle, the book, and the beach balls are all present.

Every time you notice a motivational success in your life, purchase a new copy of *The Little Engine That Could*. Give the old copy that helped you get motivated to a school, a library, or an organization that will give it to a needy child. Make sure to drop a little candle wax somewhere inside the book. Bless the wax in a way that makes you feel good about your deed.

## Considerations

- Think about how you will drip the candle wax in the books. Make certain it creates some kind of symbol that has meaning to you. Use different colors of candle wax.
- Consider writing an inscription inside the books you give away. Perhaps you can write and sign as if you are the little engine. For example: "From one engine to another engine—I know you can. The Little Engine."
- Write the initials I.T.I.C. and glue them to a photograph of a train engine. Place this photograph inside your car engine. Think about it being there whenever you need a boost.
- Gather a collection of train photos. Attach all of them to a string, and hang a sign at the bottom that says, "All of us can." Sign it "The Spirit Trains." Hang this string of trains inside your closet.

## ✦ DIRECTIVE: YELLOW PAGES POWER SPOT

Take one whole day during the weekend to accomplish this shamanic task. Begin the day by consulting the yellow pages of the phone book and looking up entries under the letter *m*. These may include entries for *machine, magazines, magician's supplies, mannequins, maps, massage, meditation, mirrors, museums*, and *musical instruments*. Choose a place that you have never visited. Make certain it arouses your curiosity. Call to make sure the place is open and then go on a drive to visit this new place.

When you arrive at the new place in your life, ask for a business card. In a notebook, write down the three most interesting things you find in the place. Ideally, these will be things you never knew existed.

When you finish with *m*, you will need to return to the yellow pages and look up the entries under the letter *o*. These may include *office equipment, oils, optical devices, organ tuning*, and *oxygen*. Choose a place and repeat the same steps as for the *m* entry.

Do this for the letters *t, i, v, a, t, i, o*, and *n*. You may find that you are only able to make one trip per day. It may take several weekends to complete the required journeys.

When you are finished, you will have visited ten new places and have ten new business cards. You will also have a notebook listing a total of thirty interesting things you found in your explorations.

From this moment on, do the following when you struggle with turning on the motivational juice. Get out your ten business cards and shuffle them like a deck of cards. Randomly select one card. That card will tell you where to go. You are to return to that place and look for the three interesting things you found there previously. If something is missing, inquire as to what happened to it. Stay in the place for at least five minutes.

The first time this exercise engages and inspires your motivation and lifts your spirit, which may be on the first try or not until later, throw away all the other cards and only keep the card of the place that helped get you motivated. From that day forward, remind yourself of that particular place whenever you need to get motivated.

Make this place your shamanic temple of motivation. The only place you will think, wonder, strategize, or do anything with your motivation will be at this special place. If you move to a different location, repeat this procedure so you can find a new motivational power spot.

## Considerations

- If you feel that your power spot needs a boost, consider finding a new place or doing something to recharge the old place. Perhaps you need to find another new thing in the place you hadn't noticed before. This time, purchase it and gift wrap it. Place it in the trunk of your car when you go on subsequent trips to the power spot.
- Find a map and mark the power spot. Write the words, "Power spot for motivation" near the marking. Place this map inside an empty bottle and leave it in an interesting place.
- Open your yellow pages to the *p* section and write in a new entry: "Power Spot." Spell out the address and phone number.
- Take someone to your power spot and tell them what you did as you walk through the place. Invite them to try it for themselves.
- Send a thank you card to the place and say, "Thank you for creating an important place. I go there to get motivated. It provides a wonderful service to the community."

✦ DIRECTIVE: DISTILLING MOTIVATIONAL EXPERTISE

Go to a place where a "motivational expert" is offering a speech or workshop on motivation. Do not attend the workshop. Instead, wait until there is a lunch break and, with a notebook in full view, talk to at least ten people who are in attendance. Ask each person you interview to tell you in one sentence the most important thing they have learned about motivation. Write these sentences down in your notebook.

Make certain you select ten different people who look motivated. Do not bother with anyone who appears unmotivated. Similarly, if someone tells you something in a manner that sounds unmotivated, it is best to reject his or her offering.

Take these ten motivational statements and type each one on a separate index card. Arrange the cards in some kind of order so that each sentence seems to be connected to the next.

Now write a letter in which you pretend to be an expert on motivation. Briefly say you have found ten important things to know about spiritual motivation and list the ten motivational statements in the order in which you arranged them. After each statement, give the name of an animal or plant you believe symbolizes the point you are making.

Send this letter to three friends who you think may be interested in shamanism. See what you can learn from their responses.

## Considerations

- Do the best statements about motivation come from those who look the most motivated?
- Consider doing the directive again and interviewing the people who look least motivated. See if there is any noticeable difference when you compare the things they say with the statements made by people who look highly motivated.
- Send a letter about your study to the motivational speaker.
- Collect photographs of the animals and plants you chose to symbolize the motivational statements. Place them in an open shoe box and consider it a shamanic nature preserve.
- Select the plant or animal that you feel is the supreme example of

motivation. Make this your private symbolic ally. Imagine talking to this ally about your motivational challenges.

## ✦ Directive: A Little Noise, Please

Go to a party store and purchase three party noisemakers. Call them Gabriel's horns and ask for their permission to be used in a shamanic way. If they do not talk back, assume they have granted their permission. Keep these shamanic noisemakers with you when you go to work. You may conceal them in a bag or briefcase.

Whenever you find yourself feeling spiritually unmotivated, go to a private place, perhaps a rest room. Take your shamanic noisemakers along with you. When no one is looking, make noise for ten seconds. Use each noisemaker. Under no circumstance should you make noise for longer than ten seconds.

After you make the noise, try to keep the memory of the sound in your head. Tell yourself that the reason you are unable to get spiritually motivated is the noise in your own head. If your mind forgets the sound of your noise, reach into your arsenal of noisemakers, pull one out, and sneak in a little reminder.

### Considerations

- Will you make one noise at a time or make all three noises at the same time?
- Recall the name of the noisemakers. When you use them, speak Gabriel's name before letting them sound off.
- Experiment with other noisemakers and names.
- Ask someone to help you. Have them make noise upon your command. Then have them direct you to make noise. Consider a duet.
- Listen to whether the world sounds the same after you make noise. Is it quieter? Calmer? Or does it seem more full of sound? Are there times when making noise makes a clearing for your mind? Study the aftereffects of making noise in this way.

## ✦ DIRECTIVE: CLUES FOR FINDING THE MISSING MOTIVATION

Before setting off on this directive, choose the task in your life that you are least motivated to accomplish. Then think of your search for motivation as a great mystery story in which someone has stolen your motivation. Pretend that some imaginary villain has stolen, kidnapped, or even murdered your motivation.

Your assignment on this case is to find ten possible clues for the crime. To create this list, you must go to your Bible or any spiritual book and randomly open it ten times to find ten sentences or verses. The only clues you can put on your list are those you actually find printed in this book.

When you have located ten possible clues, identify the one that makes the least sense to you. Write this sentence or verse on a dark piece of paper and carry it with you for at least twenty-four hours.

The next day, carefully analyze the clue and select one word from the sentence or verse. This word should be the word that is most representative of the meaning of the clue. Write that word on the palm of one of your hands.

For the next twenty-four hours, think of creating one sentence that explains the motive behind your missing motivation. This sentence must contain the word written on your hand.

The next day you may wash the word from your hand. At noon, write your sentence on a legal pad. Tear out the page it's written on and carry this sentence with you for at least a week. During that time, have a minimum of three conversations in which you explain what you did. Tell each person you simply followed some instructions from a book. Ask them to come up with an elaborate, mystical explanation for your sentence. Continue until you have collected three mystical explanations that you find interesting. They cannot be trite or obvious explanations. They must be understandings that are fascinating and bring mystery to you.

### Considerations

- Vary the spiritual books you use in the exercise. Try religious books you know nothing about or books from religions you think you wouldn't like. What surprises come forth?

- Imagine that the person who stole your motivation is a character mentioned in a religious book. Do not assume that this person stole your motivation for a bad reason. Perhaps they stole it to help you evolve spiritually.
- Pretend that the elaborate mystical explanations given to you by others actually hold deeper clues about your motivation. Examine them for clues. Choose one clue that seems to speak most directly to your curiosity. Write it down and place it in the bottom of your shoe. Take a walk and work on solving the mystery.
- Make up a motivational issue that is not a part of your life and act as if it were really an issue for you. Aim the directive at this fantasy issue.

## ✦ DIRECTIVE: DICTIONARY MEDICINE

Look up the word *motivation* in a dictionary. Choose any word the dictionary uses to define it and then look up that word. Repeat this procedure with the definition of the new word. Continue until you have worked yourself through six words in the dictionary. It doesn't matter whether you are familiar with the words you look up.

After finishing with *motivation*, repeat the process with the word *spirit*. Again work yourself through six words.

Do this every morning before you go to work, again at lunch, and then after dinner. Always begin with the words *motivation* and *spirit*. It doesn't matter if you find yourself revisiting familiar word territory. This "dictionary medicine" is to be taken three times a day for two weeks.

### Considerations

- Wait sixty seconds between looking up each word. Allow each definition to sink into your mind as a meditation.
- Randomly open the dictionary and point to any word. Imagine that it is the definition of *motivation*. Do the same for *spirit*.
- Open the dictionary ten times. Each time, write one letter of the word *motivation* across the entire page with a colored pencil. Start with the letter *m* and proceed to the next letters of the word. When

you have spelled the entire word, think of the word lying within the dictionary. Imagine it floating inside the book.

- Write down a word that you think means the opposite of motivation. Spell it backward, and consider the reverse spelling to be a motivational word.

- After you have conducted this practice at least twenty-five times, write "Dictionary Medicine" on the cover of your dictionary.

## ✦ DIRECTIVE: KNOT MOTIVATED

Go to a printing company and make an order for a minimum number of business cards for yourself. On this card, have printed only your name and the following words directly underneath your name:

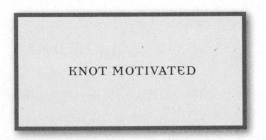

When someone asks you to do something you aren't motivated to do, immediately hand out one of these cards. Before they ask any questions, read the following to them, "Motivation is like a knot. Knots are stuck spots or lumps on an otherwise straight string or rope that sometimes bind, connect, or tie things together."

Then say, "A knot is also the name of an Old World bird, a bird that doesn't like solitude, but enjoys being with its fellow birds. Sometimes this bird was known as the 'great knot.'" Ask the person whether they have ever heard of the "great knot."

Do not discuss the card any further. Tell the person you are conducting a research project for a shamanic teacher. Your job is to ask them what they think the card means. Keep a written record of their responses.

### Considerations

- Consider someday writing a booklet or creating a Web site entitled "Knot Motivated" that includes these responses.

- Consider tying a knot in a string and carrying it with you.
- Draw a picture of a bird with this caption: "Related to the knot." When you catch yourself having motivational despair, look at this drawing and imagine that your motivational knot (the way you feel tied up or caught in an existential tangle) can fly away.
- Contemplate what it would mean to be motivated about knots. Then reexamine your new business card that says "Knot Motivated."
- Make other "Knot Motivated" cards in different sizes, colors, or designs. Remember that the knot likes company. Always carry several cards so they are never lonely.
- When you have to sign your name somewhere, add the middle name Knot.

## CONCLUDING THOUGHTS

The shamanic practices set forth in this chapter set the stage for tricking yourself into becoming motivated about those times when you are not motivated. The best method for learning how to get motivated is tinkering with the times when you can't get motivated. We don't learn a thing about how to be motivated, or become more motivated or motivated in a different way, if we remain contently motivated. Learning and growth is only possible when things aren't working. The only mistake we make when we find ourselves stuck is that we stop tinkering, experimenting, and playing. This is true not only for motivational issues, but for all human problems and suffering.

As you may be learning, the key to being a Christian shaman is accepting whatever life brings, making your prayer, walking forward with trust, and then throwing yourself into the playpen. This is why you must become like a child to enter the heavenly kingdom. Children always play with what is set in front of them. This keeps them full of vibrant energy and life. The kingdom of God is found in the sacred playpen or playground where all experiences are gifts for divine play. Praise the times when you are unmotivated. Use them to discover new and exciting pathways to becoming fully enthralled with life.

# 18

# SHAMANIC DIRECTIVES FOR ADDRESSING FEAR

*Then he said to me, do not fear, Daniel, for from the first day that you set your heart to understand, and to humble yourself before your God, your words were heard, and I have come because of your words.*

DANIEL 10:12

## SHAMANIC TEACHING

Nothing shakes us up like fear. It is a bone-rattling, skin-trembling encounter with an assumed threat to our way of being. But wouldn't it be a good thing to be able to retain the energy of fear, allowing its impact to shake us into shamanic experience, but without the negative baggage that fear brings along? Imagine that in the face of threat and death, you would tremble only with the life force.

The old ones tell us that this is our goal: to rid ourselves of the toxic fear of fear and to be receptive to the gift of energy that threat and death bring. "Keep looking over your shoulder to make sure that death is near," some of the old shamans used to say. "Keep looking to make sure that threat is all around." Fear can stretch us to live more fully. This is an old shamanic teaching.

Problems arise when we don't accept fear as bearing a gift. We try to shrink and destroy it. Again, fear makes us tremble, but so does joy.

Fear and joy are related to the trembling of life and death, the pushing and pulling of a cosmic dance. Bring forth the lunatic angels of God. Ask them to teach us the ways in which fear can be a teacher, a gift, a guide and compass for finding joy. Embrace fear in all its forms. Its serious presence will remain, but now add its absurd presence and stretch the two forms into a horizontal line, stretching yourself along with it into new realms of shamanic possibilities.

## ✦ DIRECTIVE: PEN PAL FEARS

Write the name of what you fear the most. Under the name of this fear, write the name of a fictitious person. Pretend that this person is more fearful than you are of what you named. He or she is twice as fearful as you, as hard as that may be to imagine. He or she would be greatly relieved if they could reduce their fear to the level you experience.

Your assignment is to write an imaginary letter to this fictional person. Ask them what it is like to have a fear that is twice as bad as yours. Mail this letter to your own address.

When you receive the letter, answer it as if you were the imaginary person. Write a letter to yourself describing your situation from their point of view. Mail this letter to yourself. Continue this pen pal relationship in which you write the letters for both sides of the correspondence. Over the next two months, write the letters in such a way that it appears you are actually helping the imaginary other with effective spiritual and shamanic advice. Do not cure this other person. Limit yourself to reducing the other's fear to one half of what it was originally.

### Considerations

- Rather than mailing these letters, consider leaving them in a special place in your house or apartment to be "picked up." Choose the spot in your domicile that feels least fearful to you.
- Contemplate the different kinds of advice that you might give. Perhaps you can send them one of the directives in this chapter. Write back to yourself about what happened to them when they did it.

- Give careful consideration to the stamps you put on each letter you mail. Imagine that the choice of stamp will have an unconscious influence on the imaginary other person. Furthermore, believe that the stamp is the intervention that helps them reduce their fear. Choose stamps that you believe can relieve another person's fear without their knowledge.
- Imagine that your pen pal is from another galaxy, someone who intercepts your letters and writes back to you with intelligence superior to that of any human being. Allow yourself to be influenced by their subliminal communications and therapeutic suggestions.

## ✦ DIRECTIVE: SOUND TREATMENT

Get an audio recorder and make the necessary arrangements to record your voice. The tape should be at least sixty minutes in length. Before recording, ask yourself who else has the same fear you have. It may be someone you know, someone you've heard about, or even a fictional person from a movie or novel. If you don't know anyone with the same fear, you must find someone. You can do this in any way, even finding a magazine article about someone with this fear. You may want to do a search on the Internet. When you have the name of this person, record yourself saying his or her name over and over again, for the full length of one side of the tape. Try to say the name slowly, with the same tone, intensity, and volume.

The next step is to make a list of all the spiritually oriented people you know, from the past and the present, who probably don't have this fear. Spend at least a week working on this list, making it as long as you possibly can. You can use any means to create the list. Make sure you include some biblical characters. When you have your list of people who do not share your fear, record yourself reading their names. Repeat the list, if necessary, until you have filled up the other side of the tape. Every time you utter a name, try to speak in a different way. Change your volume, the pitch of your voice, your speed of speaking, and so forth.

Wait one week before listening to the tape. At that time, you will have to make special arrangements for your listening. Obtain a portable cassette tape player that can be operated with batteries. Plan to go into a remote place, away from other people. At sunset, turn on the first side of your tape, the one on which you recorded the name of one person who shares the fear. As you listen to this side of the tape, walk away from the recorder. Keep walking until you can barely hear the tape. At the spot that marks the borderline between where you can hear and where you can no longer hear, walk back and forth between hearing and not hearing. Do this for the entire side of the tape.

Turn the tape to the other side, on which you recited many names of people who do not have the fear. Lie on the ground with your ear on the tape machine. Make sure it is at comfortable listening level, and listen to the entire side of the tape.

When the tape is finished, disassemble it. You will have to bring pliers and any other tools you might need to accomplish this part of the task. Pull out the whole tape and wrap half of it around each of your legs. Drive away from the spot with this tape around your legs. Go to a gas station and throw the tape away.

When you return home, try to refrain from thinking about what you did for two days. On the third day, send yourself a post card on which you have written these words: "I heard something important."

## Considerations

- Imagine this is the most important directive you will ever perform in your life. Find another person who will do this, while you watch and direct them. Tell them they must do it with you in order to help you.
- Choose comic book or fantasy figure names for the assignment.
- Do this directive once a year for five years. When you perform it for the last time, hold a party to celebrate your graduation.
- Write out the first paragraph of this directive and hide it in your house. Do the same for the other paragraphs, doing one each day.

✦ DIRECTIVE: THE FEAR CARD

On an index card, write down what you fear the most. On the other side of the card, write what you fear the least. Place this card inside the Book of Psalms in your Bible. Let it "sleep" there for twenty-four hours. After the card has rested, carry it with you at all times. When you find yourself becoming fearful of what you fear the most, pull out your card and stare at the side that states what you fear the least. See if you can get what you fear least to divert you from your strongest fear.

## Considerations

- Place the Bible that holds your card underneath your pillow. Sleep with it.
- Experiment with placing the card next to other verses in your Bible.
- Consider placing your Bible with the card inside next to an electrical outlet. Imagine it being charged as it rests.
- Place your Bible with the card inside next to an antenna or cable television box. Imagine it getting better reception as it rests.
- Place your Bible with the card inside between two slices of bread. Consider the spiritual meaning of this act.

## ✦ DIRECTIVE: BOTTLED-UP FEAR

Obtain a plastic bag and a glass jar large enough to contain the bag. Go to a private area and spend several minutes thinking about your fear. Place your mouth over the plastic bag and shout into it the name of your fear. You may then scream or make unusual noises into the bag, as long as they communicate everything you possibly feel about your fear. When you have exhausted the possibilities of expressing your fear, tighten the end of the plastic bag and place it into the glass jar. Immediately seal the jar and reflect on how you have bottled up your fear.

Take your bottled-up fear to a church building that looks friendly to you. Open the jar and unseal the plastic bag. Say the verse, "Fear thou not; for I am with thee."

## Considerations

- Consider that the noises you make transform your fear into raw energy that can be used in a good way by others.
- Do the directive again, this time unleashing your bottled-up fear

in a place other than a friendly church. Try a playground, a movie theater (while the movie is running), a comedy club, or a concert.

- Try opening up a plastic bag filled with fear energy and whispering a loving thought into it. Imagine the loving thought becoming stronger as it feeds upon the energy in the bag.
- Say the verse in reverse: "Thee with am I for not thou fear."
- When thinking about fear, get out a plastic bag and conduct the exercise again. This time, simply say the word "fear" as fast as you can for one minute. Try to feel fear when you do this. See how difficult this can be. Consider why this is so.

## ✦ Directive: Fear Sound Track

Obtain an audiotape recorder and record the name of your fear once every ten seconds. A ten-minute tape will contain sixty recordings of your fear's name. Make certain you say your fear in a very dramatic, fearful way. You may have to practice until you can make it sound fearful in an old-fashioned, theatrical manner.

Rent a videotape or DVD of some slapstick humor. Episodes of the Three Stooges, Charlie Chaplin, or the Marx Brothers would serve you well. Watch the videotape or DVD at the same time you play back the audiotape of your fear. Turn up the volume of your audiotape player, so you can hear your voice making a very pronounced delivery of your fear. As you watch the comedic antics, you will hear your fear sounding off every ten seconds. Watch a full ten minutes of slapstick until your audiotape has completed its job. At the end of the tape, say aloud, "There's nothing like baptizing fear in the ridiculous."

Over a period of several months, watch many silly comedies, silent film classics, and other forms of filmed lunacy while listening to your most serious effort to articulate the name of your fear.

### Considerations
- Try playing your sound track with other kinds of material—sporting events, romantic movies, news programs, and so forth.
- Ask others to perform the exercise, and play all of your recorders at the same time while watching a movie.

- Consider doing this with children. How would they respond?
- Consider doing this with your family pet. Record yourself barking in fear and then turn on a movie about an animal. Observe your pet closely.
- Imagine baptizing one person each week with laughter. Do it in your own way, but do not let others know what you are doing.

## ✦ DIRECTIVE: RICE CEREAL BOMB

Place two teaspoons of rice cereal into a small bowl. Stare at the cereal and imagine projecting your fear into the cereal, as if you had a special kind of thought power. Ask the spirit of a saint to help you do this. Hold the bowl of cereal and shake it around as if you and your saint were transmitting the vibrations of your fear into the rice.

Place this cereal into the bottom of each shoe, one teaspoon for each foot. Proceed to take a fifteen-minute walk. Feel the fearful rice cereal becoming pulverized as you walk on top of it. Imagine the crunchy sounds you would hear if your feet had ears.

After the walk, empty the rice cereal into your hand and complete the job of fully pulverizing the cereal, turning it into a powder. Place this powder into a piece of tissue paper and wrap it up. Pretend it is a bomb—a fear bomb. Go to a safe place and light the bomb. You may twist the tissue paper to make a fuse. Walk away from your bomb and listen to hear whether or not there is a loud explosion. Judge the power of your fear by the loudness of the explosion.

### Considerations

- Try staring at the cereal in the dark. Imagine that this makes the thought power stronger.
- Secretly pour a small amount of the pulverized cereal at the entry to a church. After a Sunday service, return to see if any powder remains.
- Eat some rice cereal after conducting this task.
- Keep a box of rice cereal in every room of your house while you conduct this work.

- Consider sending a box of rice cereal to the most fearful person you know.

## ✦ DIRECTIVE: FEAR PETS

Go to a toy store and purchase two stuffed animals. One should be the most frightening stuffed toy you can find and the other should be completely nonfrightening. At first, keep the two animals separate from one another. Keep the scary one in a closet and keep the nonfrightening one on top your bed, near your pillow.

For five minutes before you go to sleep, go into your closet and pet the frightening animal. Pretend it is afraid to be seen by other animals because everyone thinks it looks scary. Pet it and believe you are providing comfort. Say a little prayer for it. Do this every night for a week. This will give the animal courage to come out of the closet.

After a week of building courage, present the closet animal with a piece of your clothing that you find comforting and attractive. With this piece of clothing, bring out the closet animal and set it next to the other animal on your bed. Every evening before you go to sleep, do the following with the two creatures. Have the nonfrightening animal pet the other animal and say a prayer for it. Let it help build up the other's courage in the same way you helped it before.

After another week has passed, place the two animals in your closet together. For the rest of the year, pet each animal just before you go to sleep and make a small prayer. If you have to go out of town, give them some extra care and attention before you leave.

### Considerations

- Consider making animal sounds before each prayer. Think of this as a shamanic way of joining your new friends.
- Name the animals. Use these names in your prayers.
- Instead of petting them, try scratching the animals to relieve an itch they have.
- For one night, stand underneath your shower with both animals. Have the nonfrightening one pet and encourage the other one

as described earlier. At the end, turn the water on for a second. Everyone should end up wet.

- Place the animals in the passenger seat of your car and drive to a special, private place. Give them each a small Bible when you arrive. From that day on, make sure that they are always with their Bibles.

## ✦ DIRECTIVE: FEAR BALLS

Take a sheet of paper and write the name of your fear at the top. Then list everything you can think of that describes your experience of the fear. Go to a copy shop and make thirty-three copies of this sheet of fear. Take the copies home and wad each paper into a paper ball. You will have a total of thirty-three "fear balls."

Carry this supply of fear balls with you throughout the next week. Whenever you begin thinking about your fear, get out a fear ball, go to the nearest trash can, and slam it into the can. Say to yourself, "In the name of Christian shamanism, so much for that fear ball!"

### Considerations

- See how many fear balls you can successfully throw into your home trash can by the end of the day. See if the number of successful baskets influences how you feel when you wake up the next morning.
- Keep the sheet on which you originally wrote your fear separate from the copied sheets. Call it "the original fear ball." Consider the other thirty-three fear balls to be practice balls. After you have thrown them away, take a deep breath and drop the original fear ball into the basket. Believe that this is the one that counts.
- Carry one fear ball with you for each day of the month. Throw it away before you go to bed.
- At the end of the month, throw each fear ball away in a different trash can outside of your home.
- Consider wrapping all the fear balls into one large fear ball. Wrap it with tape and roll it around your house before throwing it away for good.

## ✦ Directive: Fear Power

To the best of your abilities, draw a picture of your fear. Feel free to be very abstract and wild in your artistic rendering. Take the drawing and rub it against a page of Revelations. Make sure the page makes reference to scary images or events. Now when you find yourself struggling with someone you fear, go to this fear picture and rub it three times with your little finger.

The next time you see the person who intimidated you, wave that little finger at him or her. Know that there is great power in the finger that rubbed against the spiritually energized picture.

### Considerations

- Consider making a sand painting and pouring the sand onto a page of Revelations. Pour the sand into a jar and keep it available for charging your finger.
- After drawing the picture of your fear, burn it. Rub some of the ashes against a page of Revelations. Use this page to activate your finger.
- Place one drop of river water on your finger. Rub it into Revelations. Only point that finger when absolutely necessary.
- Blow across the page of Revelations and allow the wind to hit the specific finger. Proceed as before.
- Cut out one word from a page of Revelations. Place it beneath a bandage and attach it to your fingertip. Use this when you need an extra boost of power.

## ✦ Directive: Once Upon a Time . . .

This directive is different from the others in that it begins with a story.

Once upon a time there lived a princess who was very fearful that her fear would never go away. She worried at least twelve hours a day that her fear would sneak up on her and give her a fright. One day she couldn't stand it any longer. She screamed out, as loudly as she could, "Get out of my life!" She looked at the sky and begged God to take away her fear.

Within seconds, a cricket landed in the palm of her hand. She thought she heard it making a sound. Bringing it close to her ear, she heard that it was actually crying, making the sound a little child produces when hurt. "What's wrong?" asked the princess. The cricket responded, "It was me you feared. You asked me to go away and it hurt my feelings. Now I'm stuck in the outer world. You wouldn't let me live in peace in the inner world, so here I am in your hand."

The rest of the story takes many hours to tell, but for our purposes it is enough to know that the princess and the cricket became best friends and remained together until the very last day of the princess's life. After she died, the court jester found a letter she had written, with instructions for it to be opened one hundred years after her death. The letter stated:

> *Your fear is inside you. Make it your friend. If you don't, it will think you are going to leave it alone. You will then feel its fear. You will feel how frightened it is by the possibility of being left alone. Remember that God loves all the creatures of the outside and inside worlds, including the creature called fear. In my case, my fear almost left me. If it had, I would have felt very lonely. Fortunately, it became a magic cricket that lived with me throughout my life. It told me to tell you this. Go purchase the metal toy that makes the sound of a cricket. Keep it in with you at all times. If you ever feel the fear inside you, just give it a click. This will help your fear know that you are there with it and it doesn't have to be afraid.*

Now, get yourself a clicker and perform a ritual to prepare it for this task. Do this by reading it the story of the princess and the cricket each night for three days. Beginning the next day, carry the clicker with you. Whenever you feel any fear, give it a click. Like the story, remind your fear that it doesn't have to be afraid.

## Considerations

- Draw a cricket and attach it to your hammer. Hammer a nail into a board and say aloud, "Damn, what a noise this cricket can make!"

- Imagine that you carry a clicker and go through the motions of clicking it while making the clicking sound yourself.
- Find out how a cricket makes its sound. Tell at least one person each week what you've learned.
- After you say your evening prayer, make the clicking sound. Consider this a new "Amen."

## CONCLUDING THOUGHTS

Fear can immobilize us as its intensity threatens to throw our system into emotional shock. No challenge presents itself with as powerful a tool for personal transformation and growth than raw naked fear. Embrace fear and wrestle it to the ground with equally intense and extreme absurdity. Whether you have rice cereal in your shoes, a fear card in your pocket, or fear balls to throw in the air, know that fear presents a radical opportunity for really jumping off the deep end. When fear strikes, don't hold back. Dig deeper into the trickster's arsenal and meet it head on. Dance with it, tickle it, and invite it to come into your playground. Fear can transform the deepest parts of you. It can bring the biggest release of humor and open the doors to the deepest calm.

Behind every extreme is a door that takes you to its opposite form. Stretch fear with absurd play and find yourself entering the ecstatic currents of spiritual delight. Cultivate an awareness of how many times you meet fear and tap into its energy. Stare fear in the face and don't run away from it (unless it is appropriate to do so for personal safety). Look for fear's funny bone. Tickle it and watch yourself become what fear fears most. Consider how fear runs away from the fully developed Christian shaman. It loses face when it instantly transforms from serious fright to a lighthearted joke. Let these lessons teach you the power of conquering fear with a single feather solely used for tickling the situation at hand.

# 19

# SHAMANIC DIRECTIVES
# FOR ADDRESSING
# INSOMNIA

*Yet a little sleep, a little slumber, a little folding of the hands to sleep.*

PROVERBS 6:10

## SHAMANIC TEACHING

Night is a garden for the spirit. Recognize it as a time to plant seeds for the harvest of spiritual dreams. If you are unable to sleep, consider this a time of preparation for the shamanic garden of the night, a time to till the soil and act as a steward of the dream landscape. As you lie awake, consider pretending to dream, dreaming yourself into dreaming. We sometimes worry about not sleeping. Is it better to be concerned over the planting and the harvesting, whether one is awake or asleep?

No matter what challenge you face, even insomnia, know that the winds of absurdity are available, ready to stretch any shrunken serious concern with the help of its partner, absurd play. Awaken the merriment of trickster wisdom, permitting it to enter the challenges of the night. Being awake is a classroom for learning how to prepare for the entry into dream, as dream should be the preparation for entry into the waking trance of the everyday.

## ✦ DIRECTIVE: WATER LULLABY

Fill every glass you own with water and place these full glasses around your bed. When you retire for the evening, take a spoon and tap every glass so you hear it ring. Keep the ringing sound in your mind as you get into bed. Lie there imagining that the glasses are playing music all around you. Fantasize seeing a tiny angel flying from glass to glass, making the most beautiful music ever heard.

As you listen to this night music, try to turn it into a lazy lullaby. If you are unable to slow the music, get up and empty some of the water out of one of the glasses. (You will have to take the glass to the kitchen or bathroom.) Before going back to bed, sound each glass again with your spoon. Begin the music in your mind and try again to get that slow lullaby. Repeat the procedure over and over, emptying more and more water from different glasses, until the music is right. The right music will be a slow, hypnotic lullaby that comforts you into not caring whether or not you fall asleep.

### Considerations

- Consider surrounding your bed with stones that you tap with a hammer before going to bed. Listen to the tapping sounds. Can you imagine an angel gently tap dancing around you?
- Place your favorite tapes or compact discs in a circle around your bed. Think of the music they hold as you retire.
- Open your favorite books and place them in a circle around your bed. Imagine their wisdom floating from the pages and entering your mind as you become relaxed.
- Write the words "sacred sleep" on soothing-colored paper. Place these sheets around your bed and sprinkle water on them before retiring.
- Write down every dream you can remember having on separate sheets of paper. If you can't remember them, make up some dreams you wish you could have, or go get a book on dreams and write down some of the dreams you like from the book. Place these around your bed. Call it your "dream circle."

## ✦ DIRECTIVE: SAND AND AIR

Fill a small jar with sand. Five minutes before going to bed, open your jar of sand and place your fingers, one by one, into the bed of sand. As each finger goes into the sand, quietly say to yourself, "Now I lay me down to sleep." Pretend that the sand puts your fingers into a state of complete relaxation.

Do this every night with a new jar until the entire area under your bed is filled with little jars of sand. When the task is complete, think about all the sand underneath your bed as often as you can during the day. In the evening, try not to think of the sand.

For every evening of peaceful sleep you receive, empty one jar of sand into a bucket that you keep in the closet. Place the empty jar underneath the bed. You will now begin creating more and more little jars full of air.

Throughout the day, think of this air and the sand sitting next to it. Again, try not to think of the air or the sand or the jars during the evening.

### Considerations

- Think about places in the world that contain a great deal of sand—from Caribbean beaches to the Kalahari and Sahara Deserts. While resting over your bedroom sand, ask yourself if you are sleeping on a beach, a desert, or both.
- Experiment with various placements of the jars under your bed. Do you arrange them in symbolic patterns?
- Before going to bed, lie down on the floor next to your bed and stare at your jars for five minutes. Decide whether or not you will speak to them.
- Take a bottle of sand and a bottle of air with you to work. When you need to catch a brief nap or a moment of relaxation, take them out and set them in front of you.

## ✦ DIRECTIVE: EARLY THEORIES OF SLEEP

Ask several parents who have young children to do you a favor. Have them ask their children how it is that a person is able to go to sleep.

Write down all the answers you get and study them. Know them by heart, and begin a collection of children's theories on sleeping. Remind yourself that children have a special spiritual sensitivity, whether or not they are aware of it.

When you go to sleep, think of the many theories about sleep you have learned from these young teachers. Be grateful that your evening experiences have awakened you to the enchanting ideas of children.

## Considerations

- Write down the names of several of your childhood friends. Imagine the sleep theories each might have come up with when they were children.
- Ask children about their dreams and what they think the dreams mean.
- Make up a dream you believe you could have had as a child. Guess what your childhood best friend might have said it meant.
- Ask a child to draw a picture of a dream he or she had. Ask him or her to give the dream a name. Draw your own conclusions as to how the name of the child's dream explains the dream.
- Ask a child to imagine what kind of dreams dogs and cats have.

## ✦ DIRECTIVE: REJOICING IN RELIEF

When you are unable to get to sleep, get up and lie down on the floor. You may use a blanket to keep you warm. Feel how long it takes before your body begins to feel uncomfortable. What part of you begins to ache first? As you experience the growing discomfort, think how good it will feel to get back into your bed. Do not allow yourself to return to the comfort of the mattress until you absolutely cannot take any more discomfort.

When you must get up, turn on a flashlight and write down the parts of your body that ache the most and are most relieved to get off the floor. After each body part you name, write, "Thank you, Jesus. I rejoice in getting up." Go to bed thinking only of those parts of your body and rejoicing with the words, "Thank you." Imagine they will go to sleep in a happy way, even if the rest of you is not appreciative. Lie there reflecting on a body that is already happy with how certain parts feel.

## Considerations

- Consider which parts of your body are happiest about receiving relief from discomfort. Call those parts your "happy zones." Are these the parts of your body that are most likely to become uncomfortable?
- Is discomfort a precondition for comfort? Think about this.
- Consider focusing on a previously unnoticed part of your body. Can you make it uncomfortable and then provide it with relief?
- See if you can pretend to be uncomfortable when you are not. Will that skill enable you to pretend to be comfortable when you are uncomfortable?
- Say "thank you" whenever you become aware that any part of your body is feeling different, whether it is becoming comfortable or uncomfortable. Contemplate how noticing the difference is an indication or communication that you are alive.
- Write a letter to your body's happy zones. Ask them to teach the rest of your body to be as alive as they are.

## ✦ DIRECTIVE: BACKWARD SLEEP

Before retiring, spend thirty minutes reading the Bible backward. Start at the end and read each sentence in the reverse direction. Say the name of Jesus backward, "Susej."

Change out of your daytime clothes and then put your clothes on again. Repeat this undressing and dressing for six cycles. Each time say, "Susej."

Go to the kitchen, get an empty glass, and pretend you're drinking the air that is inside it. Then fill it up with water and leave the glass on the countertop. Do not drink it or pour it out. Say "Susej."

Go to your bed and pull the covers back. Count backward from ten to zero and then make up the bed. Do this five times. Don't forget to say, "Susej."

When you get into your bed, do not allow any of your thoughts to go forward. Everything in your mind must be done backward. Repeat "Susej."

Say quietly to yourself, "I hope I stay awake tonight and get a good night of wakefulness. After all, it would teach me a lot about being backward." Then say, "Susej."

## Considerations

- While doing these shamanic exercises, focus on the Japanese proverb, "For every truth, the opposite is also true."
- Sign your name backward in some minor transaction.
- Begin the day by reversing the way you brush your teeth.
- End the evening by standing up in bed for a minute.
- Ask your unconscious to have a dream that mixes you up.

## ✦ DIRECTIVE: PRETEND SLEEP

Go to bed and pretend you have fallen asleep. Pretend to sleep for at least half an hour. After the required pretend sleep, get up out of bed and pretend to sleep walk. Squint your eyes, allowing enough visibility for careful navigation, putting your arms straight out like Frankenstein, and walk around the house for at least ten minutes. Do not open your eyes fully or let your arms down. All eating and entertainment are off limits. You are restricted to doing the best job you can of walking in your sleep. Return to bed and pretend you are reading the Bible. Pretend to say a prayer, but remain silent. Lie down and think about pretending to be awake. Enjoy any confusion that may come upon you. Accept it as an advanced shamanic teaching.

## Considerations

- After doing this directive for at least three nights, one evening simply pretend that you did it. Lie in bed and imagine going through all the steps.
- When you pretend to read the Bible, make nonsense sounds as you conduct your pretend reading.

- While walking in your sleep, decide whether you will walk in straight lines or circles. Experiment with different walking patterns.
- As you walk in your sleep with outstretched arms, hold a Bible in one hand and a candle in the other. Decide for yourself whether the candle will be lit or unlit.
- Wake up in the morning and pretend that you didn't do any of the above, but simply dreamed of doing it.

## ✦ DIRECTIVE: SLEEP SANDWICH

Have another person trace the outline of your whole body on a large piece of paper. Do this twice, so you end up with two full-scale body outlines. On one body write the words *deep sleep* as many times as it takes to fill in the entire space inside the outline. Place this "deep sleep body" under the part of your bed in which you sleep. On the other body write the word *dreams* as many times as it takes to fill up the outline. Attach this "dream body" to the ceiling immediately above the part of the bed in which you sleep.

When you retire for the evening, reflect on how you are the middle of a "sleep sandwich." You are located midway between deep sleep and dreams. Imagine seeing the deep sleep body below you floating up into your own body on the bed. At the same time, see the dream body above you floating down into the middle body. Let all three of these body images merge into one another in as many different ways as you can imagine.

## *Considerations*

- Consider painting each of the two bodies a different color. Which color would you choose for deep sleep and which for dreaming?
- Tie a string to the belly button of the dream body and let it hang all the way to the bed so it rubs against you as you sleep. Attach a string to the belly button of the deep sleep body and attach one end to the bed mattress or springs underneath.
- If you get hungry in the middle of the night, make yourself an edible sleep sandwich. Think of what bread, cracker, or other food will be the top, bottom, and middle slices. Think of your bedroom dream sandwich as you eat your kitchen dream sandwich. If you are on a diet, don't eat more than one bite.

- Think of other bodies you could create besides the deep sleep and dream bodies. How many layers can you imagine?
- Before going to sleep, make a prayer to have a dream of entering a Holy Ghost body that will provide spiritual teaching through osmosis.

## CONCLUDING THOUGHTS

Don't use the word "insomnia." Instead, refer to this kind of situation as a time when the difference between sleep and waking is being stretched. Sleep and waking are stretched when you want to sleep, but can't seem to do so. Rather than fighting the stretch, flow with it. The shamanic way to meet this situation is to join with the stretching and stretch it further. The further the difference between sleep and waking is stretched, the more likely you will make a transformation, which may include deep sleep.

Enter the stretch and play with the difference between sleep and waking. See how much you can learn in this play of contrary states of consciousness. The Christian shaman prays not only "Lay me down to sleep" but also "Lead me into playing with sleep, waking, and the differences that lie between." The latter is the shamanic garden where mysterious seeds are harvested in the night.

# 20

# SHAMANIC DIRECTIVES
# FOR ADDRESSING
# SELF-CONTROL

*For whatever a person succumbs to, to that he is enslaved.*

2 PETER 2:19

## SHAMANIC TEACHING

The more human beings have tried to control nature, the more out of control both have become. This pertains to both our inner and outer natures. Taoism teaches that we should not push against the grain or purposely try to make things happen. It teaches us to join with the natural currents of life and surrender ourselves to the Greater Mind that is nature itself.

For the Christian shaman, the same Taoist surrender is voiced through the prayer, "Let it be Thy will." There is no better shamanic classroom than facing the stubborn problematic habits that have become part of our lives and committing ourselves to shamanic experimentation with them. Consider this work your basic shamanic laboratory.

A habit that is problematic often takes the form of excess—excessive smoking, drinking, napping, fooling around, or shopping, to name a few possibilities. Some problematic habits come in the opposite form—you don't spend enough time and energy on something that you wish to address, whether studying, practicing, or working out. Whatever your habit structure, you can begin addressing the habits that concern you in a shamanic way. As before, you will take the serious concern and stretch it toward absurdity, helping bring forth the horizontal arm of the cross.

## ✦ DIRECTIVE: LET ME COUNT THE WAYS

The next time you're tempted by a temptation—a habit you feel you pursue in excess—immediately go to the phone book and open it up. Randomly select a residential phone number and dial it. When you get an answer, ask the following question, "Do you sell _____?" (Fill in the name of whatever is tempting you.) Reflect on the response to your inquiry. Are you told, "No, you have the wrong number"? Or does the person silently hang up? Consider how many ways there are to say no and to correct mistakes.

### *Considerations*

- You may want to consider not fully dialing the number. Dial every digit but the last one and then hang up. Pause and think about how the person may have responded.
- You can choose to only call businesses listed in the yellow pages, rather than individuals listed in the white pages.
- Purchase a toy phone and pretend to call important people in the world to ask them if they sell your temptation. Try calling the president of a country, a renowned spiritual leader, or a famous biblical character from the past.
- Get a tin can and attach a string to it. Run the string outside your bedroom window and tie it to a tree. Imagine that you are calling the tree.
- Try doing the exercise in Morse code. Tap the name of the temptation with dots and dashes.

## ✦ DIRECTIVE: HOLY NO'S

Go to a business supply or hardware store and purchase two large letters, *n* and *o*. Then go to a religious store and purchase two tiny crosses. Attach each letter to one of the crosses. Place one lettered cross in one pocket and the other lettered cross in another pocket. Carry these with you at all times, knowing that you are always carrying a spiritual "no" with you.

## Considerations

- Consider doing this with extremely small letters and crosses.
- When you sleep, place a cross at the top and bottom of your bed. Sleep inside a "holy no."
- Create another "holy no" for a friend who will appreciate this kind of shamanic work. Go someplace together where you can both carry your crosses and use them in a beneficial way.
- When you feel that you have acquired a strong and effective way of saying no, make yourself a "holy yes" in the same manner. This will require three letters and three crosses.
- Consider how you will carry your "holy yes." Might you carry a letter in each pocket and tape the third lettered cross over your heart?
- After becoming comfortable carrying your "holy yes," practice carrying both your "yes" and your "no." You may have to get creative to find enough places on your body to carry all five crosses and letters.

## ✦ DIRECTIVE: SHAMANIC SQUIRT

Purchase a squirt gun. Fill it with water you have blessed with a prayer, place it in a plastic food bag, and carry it with you to a social situation. At an inappropriate but safe time, squirt a friend. Before they say anything, tell them you're sorry, but you're trying to practice controlling your impulses. Say no more. If they ask you why you can't say more, tell them this, too, is part of learning to control your impulses.

## Considerations

- What prayer will you say to bless the water? Consider a three-word blessing, a twelve-word blessing, and a paragraph-long blessing. Write them down and have them available for the blessing recitation.
- What source of water will you use? Try finding and purchasing different bottled waters from around the world. Perhaps you might look up where a particular saint lived, and find a bottled

water that comes from a region close to a place at which he or she performed a miracle or had a vision.

- Rather than squirting a friend, squirt a plant or a rock or a building. Don't forget to apologize and explain your action.
- Before going to work in the morning, squirt yourself. Immediately say, "I'm ready for the day."

## ✦ Directive: Walking with the Dead

Arrange to walk around the outside of a church or cemetery. Walk at your normal speed and time yourself. Stop when you've walked five minutes and return to where you started (total normal walking time: ten minutes).

The next day, take the same walk, but stretch it to twelve minutes—walk six minutes in one direction and six minutes back. You may not exceed the distance you went the day before, so you will have to slow down. Repeat until you can do the walk naturally in twelve minutes.

### Considerations

- For the first five minutes, look at the cemetery. When you return, try not to look at it or think about it. Look to the other side.
- Hum a church hymn as you do your walk. Adjust the tempo so that it is in sync with your steps.
- Try another cemetery. Make it a fifteen-minute walk that becomes a twenty-minute walk with practice.
- At the end of the walk, consider saying a prayer for the souls who rest in peace.
- Take a photograph of the cemetery. Try walking somewhere else while carrying the photograph. Pretend you are walking around the cemetery.

## ✦ Directive: Wave Reading

Read a spiritual essay at a much slower rate than what you're accustomed to.

The next evening, read the same thing at a slower rate than you did the day before.

## Considerations

- When you read at a slower rate, underline the important ideas. Take your time underlining and do it more slowly than you ever have before. The next evening, underline the important ideas at an even slower pace, using a different color marker.
- Alternate reading rates for each paragraph. Read one paragraph quickly and the next one slowly. Continue reading in this way. Call it "wave reading."
- Arrange to have two sources of reading material—a spiritual essay and an unspiritual essay (however you define the latter). Read one paragraph of the spiritual essay at a slow rate and then read a paragraph of the unspiritual essay at a fast rate. Practice variations of this exercise.
- Read the first paragraph of a spiritual essay slowly. Then read the last paragraph quickly. Return to the second paragraph for a slow read, then go to the next to last paragraph for a fast read. Continue until the two reading directions meet in the middle. Cut out that paragraph and carry it with you for a while. Consider that this paragraph holds an important clue for your spiritual development.
- Write a special prayer about keeping in rhythm with the spirit. Say it aloud, but alternate the speed of your speech for every other sentence.

## ✦ DIRECTIVE: SOUL WHISPERER

When you're in a stressful social situation talking with someone, do the following:

Reach over as if you're making an adjustment to your shoe, and whisper, "I'm spiritually adjusting myself." Make certain that no one can hear this but you. Repeat the process at least three different times, each time in a different situation.

## Considerations

- Every once in a while, say, "I'm spiritually de-adjusting myself." After doing so, adjust the other shoe and say, "Now I'm getting spiritually adjusted again."

- Rather than adjusting your shoe, calibrate your watch. Take it off and set the time five minutes ahead of the correct time. After five minutes, adjust it back to the accurate time.
- Don't forget to mumble the magic words.
- Consider tapping your head three to five times while saying silently, "I'm spiritually tuning myself."
- Purchase a tuning knob from Radio Shack and carry it with you. Turn it when you need an adjustment.
- Pretend that your cell phone buzzed you. Open it and pretend to listen. Say aloud in front of the other person so that he or she can hear, "No problem, I'll adjust the situation. It's always possible for things to get better. Thanks. See you later." Then hang up.

## ✦ Directive: Hidden Blessing

Write down the following message on a piece of paper: "Bless this moment: I am managing what others see." Fold it neatly and hide it in your room or office, making sure it is out of everyone's sight.

### *Considerations*

- Consider placing it in a menu at a restaurant.
- Hide it in a phone booth—inside the phone book, taped to the ceiling, or elsewhere.
- Place it in a public toilet stall.
- Place it inside a church hymnbook or Bible.
- Hide it in a psychotherapist's office.

## ✦ Directive: Keeping Track of Yes and No

Carry a pad of paper and a pen with you at all times. Make a mark every time you hear the word *no*. At the end of each day, add up how many no's you heard. Write down that number, fold it up, and use it as a spiritual offering. Do this for at least a week, keeping track of how many no's you collect each day.

## Considerations

- Note the time of day at which you have accumulated a dozen no's.
- Note which day of the week has the most no's. Consider saying fewer no's on that day of the following week.
- Which day has the fewest no's? Consider whether you will try to say more no's on that day next week.
- Drop the folded-up numbers in an offering plate. Be sure to add some money in order to balance your action.
- Do the same exercise for the word *yes*. Find out where, when, and how yes's appear in your world.

## ✦ DIRECTIVE: SPICING UP AND NAILING DOWN THE TEACHING

Go to the grocery store and buy a spice you would never eat. Carry this spice with you as you go to a hardware store. There, purchase a nail, particularly one that seems different in some way from the others.

Carry the spice and the nail with you and go to a religious bookstore. Leave the spice and nail on a shelf near a book in which you limit yourself to reading one page.

## Considerations

- Consider returning to the religious bookstore each day to see what happened to the spice and nail. Read another page of the book at each visit.
- Repeat the exercise. This time, simply sprinkle a tiny bit of the spice on your hand before you open the book. Rub the nail when you put the book back on the shelf. Make three visits so that you will have read three pages of the book in this shamanic fashion.
- Try the directive in this way: First, find a book you are curious about. Then go find a spice that seems to be appropriate for the particular book. Determine the length of nail that is appropriate for the book (for example, long books may require longer nails). Now go back to the book with your spice and nail and whisper to the book what you have done. Make sure someone is watching, but don't be too overt.

- Buy a spice with which you are unfamiliar and then purchase an unusual nail. Take them with you as you search for what you would consider an unusual book. This may be a nonspiritual book, or a book from another spiritual tradition.

## ✦ DIRECTIVE: ERASE IT

Using a tape recorder, record your voice speaking the names of as many temptations as you can think of. Go to every room of your house with this tape. Stand in each room for exactly five minutes, holding the tape, but do not play it! Say only, "With an honoring of Abraham, I stand here now."

The next day, go back to each room with your tape and tape recorder. Erase the entire tape once in each room—erasing it again and again as you visit each room. Don't forget to verbally honor Abraham in each room.

### Considerations

- Tape yourself saying the word "temptation" over and over again. Then erase it. Do this every day for a week.
- Purchase a cheap microphone and carry it with you. When you face a temptation, get out your microphone and hold it in front of the temptation. Say nothing, and then walk away to write down your experience of the procedure.
- Get a cassette tape and wrap it with packing tape. Wrap it again with another kind of tape. Wrap it with as many different kinds of tape as you can find. Consider this the taped tape. Make one for every temptation in your life.
- Carry a tape recorder with you for a full day. Do not use it. Say nothing about it. If anyone asks, say, "It's really nothing" or "It's not as interesting as it seems." When you think about why you are doing this, say to yourself, "It's really nothing" or "It's not as interesting as it seems."
- Send a brand-new, unopened, blank tape to a friend who appreciates strange experiences. Ask them if they have heard this tape before. Tell them you were tempted to tell them what was on it, but didn't give in to the temptation.

✦ DIRECTIVE: SPREADING AND UNSPREADING THE WORD

When you get up in the morning, write down on a piece of paper something you wish you could tell a friend about Christian shamanism. Immediately throw this paper away and go on with your day.

## Considerations

- What people would you like to share some of your knowledge of Christian shamanism with? Include people from the past.
- Write a letter to Jesus and ask him three questions about Christian shamanism. Address the letter to Jesus, The Heavenly Kingdom. Place a stamp on it and place it under your pillow.
- Pretend you have a temptation to place the letter in a church offering plate, but do not do so.
- Write the words *Christian Shaman* in your Bible, as if it were your name. Write over it every day, so that you write the words many times. Believe that this is making you stronger. As the words get heavier with ink, your spiritual muscle gets more developed. Think of this strength when you need it.
- Tell a friend something about Christian shamanism that you feel they would not understand. Interrupt yourself when you are halfway through your presentation. Do not allow them to convince you to complete what you were going to say.
- Write C.S. after your signature once a day. Do not allow yourself to do it more than once each day.

✦ DIRECTIVE: TV SPIRITUALITY

At the beginning of the week, examine the television program listings and select one program you have never seen. Watch only five minutes of this program. Read a randomly selected biblical scripture. After this, return to your everyday viewing habits.

## Considerations

- Is a television program more or less interesting if you hold your Bible or a cross or a powerful symbol while watching it?

- Call your own phone number while watching a television program. If you don't have a cell phone, call your own number from a friend's house. When it is time to leave a message, read every other word of a Bible verse. Listen to this message before you go to bed.
- After reading the Bible verse, ring a bell three times. Turn the television off and on three times, and then return to your viewing.
- For one minute, watch an evangelical television show that you feel is a sham. Mail them one cent and consider how much it will cost them to handle that penny. Encourage others to do the same. See this as a way of helping curb their temptation to be rich.

## CONCLUDING THOUGHTS

The Christian shaman, like everyone else, must confront temptations and issues of self-control. For the shaman, however, these can become times for merry play and radical tinkering. Doing anything different with a habit structure can be transformative—whether it is changing how long a behavior lasts, where it takes place, any of its ordered sequences, its color, sound, audience, and so forth. Doing so with the spirit of play empowers the shamanic work. It lightens the situation and facilitates a stretching toward new possibilities.

Problem habits just seem to drop into our lives for no reason. They are like random inserts into the flow of everyday living. They need no reason for their placement in our lives. They are just there and we find ourselves stuck for no reason at all. The shaman meets this absurd situation with counterabsurdity. For no reason at all, the stuck habits are met with random acts of nonsense and tomfoolery. This engagement of chaos and illogical encounter helps undo the stuck doings, freeing us for other ways of dancing through the next chapters of life.

# 21

# SHAMANIC DIRECTIVES FOR ADDRESSING WEIGHT CONTROL

*Then God said, "I give you every seed-bearing plant on
the face of the whole earth and every tree that has fruit
with seed in it. They will be yours for food."*

GENESIS 1:29

*Everything that lives and moves will be food for you. Just
as I give you the green plants, I now give you everything."*

GENESIS 9:3

*Strengthen me with raisins, refresh me with apples, for I
am faint with love.*

SOLOMON 2:5

## SHAMANIC TEACHING

There's only one word you need to know to stop eating too much: "Stop!"
But that doesn't work. If it did, the best-selling diet book would be one
page long and have only one word. Diets obviously don't work, but the
multi-billion-dollar diet industry keeps churning out more diet books and
programs, each with the promise, "This time it will really work."

The wisest shamans I have known say that all diets are out of step with the way life works. Diets ignore the fact that the body is constantly changing, that what is best for it at one moment may be wrong for it the next moment. The wisest shamans have only one teaching about diet: "Learn to listen to what your body wants. Your body is trying to tell you what it needs, and it may change its requests from meal to meal, from day to day." Unfortunately, we hear taped loops in our heads coming from habituated assumptions. That noise blocks us from hearing what our body is trying to tell us. It is up to us to learn to stop this internal diet propaganda.

Still your mind so you can hear the whispering of your body. It is the only diet doctor that you need. The shamanic path to changing bad eating habits is to join with them and stretch them toward absurdity. Doing so will help open the door to your deeper voice, the sound of your body gently directing you to choose the foods it needs for nutrition and sustenance.

## ✦ DIRECTIVE: BEING ON TOP OF THINGS

Stand on a ladder and eat a meal from the top of your refrigerator. With each bite say, "I'm not eating everything beneath my fork. Thank you for this lofty spiritual oversight."

### *Considerations*

- Read one Bible passage in this same manner. Stand on your ladder with the Bible on top of the refrigerator. Afterwards say, "May this wisdom help preserve the world below."
- Write down a Bible verse. Place it in your freezer. Wait three days, and then take the verse out of the freezer that morning after getting up. Think about this verse thawing out during the day. After dinner, stand on the ladder and read it slowly and carefully.
- Experiment with the placement of Bible verses in your freezer and refrigerator. Which ones get frozen? Which ones belong with the vegetables, which ones with the milk, and which ones with the meat?
- Remove a frozen Bible verse from your freezer. Place it in an ice chest filled with ice. Take it to a picnic area. Sit on the ground and open your chest, carefully removing the verse. Sit with this verse for twenty minutes, meditating on its importance and deeper meanings.

- With a knife, carve a short Bible verse onto a piece of food that you have in your refrigerator. Wait twenty-four hours and then eat it with a reverent attitude.

## ✦ DIRECTIVE: THE ONE

Try to gain exactly one pound in seven days. Consider what you will learn about weight control by gaining an exact amount of weight. Do not, under any circumstances, try to lose weight until you can accurately gain one pound in one week.

### Considerations

- When you successfully gain one pound, spiritually reward yourself with a minibaptism. Sprinkle yourself with a few drops of water that you have previously prayed over. Say, "With these drops, I honor the One."
- Next, write down how many pounds you want to lose on the back of a compass. Make sure you are facing north whenever you eat. See this as placing yourself in a receptive spiritual direction.
- Make a vow to not say the word *pound* for a month. Refer to weight in terms of miles. For example, one pound becomes one mile, and two pounds becomes two miles. Stop saying that you want to lose ten pounds. Say instead that you want to travel ten miles. See your diet as a spiritual journey.
- Go to a bookstore and examine the photos of authors who have written diet books. Select the photo that you believe shows a spiritually strong person. Purchase that book. Do not read it. Simply look at the photograph of the author before each meal.
- Ask your body permission before trying to alter its mass. Do this before each meal.

## ✦ DIRECTIVE: STRAW PERSON

Drink a glass of your favorite beverage using as many straws as you can. The next day, drink the same beverage with one less straw. Repeat each day until you have no straws left.

Pretend you learned something from this exercise. Write down what you did, what you learned, and what others can learn from your experience. Leave this account in a church hymnbook.

## Considerations

- After each drinking session, tape the withdrawn straw to the straw from the previous day. When the task is completed and all the straws are connected, measure the length of the new straw. Consider this length to be the distance you must travel to lose your desired amount of weight.
- Take your long straw and place it next to your Bible. Imagine that it is a spiritual antenna that draws upon higher-level wisdom. Open your Bible to a scripture while using this antenna. Think of the verse as holding a clue for your diet.
- Consider the long straw to be a new source of spiritual backbone for you. Give it an appropriate offering.
- Hold onto the long straw in your prayers.

## ✦ Directive: Double Time

Place two forks on top of each other and tape them together. Say two prayers before eating your next meal. Use the double fork and double prayer until you've learned something about your eating habits.

## Considerations

- Let the first word to come out of your mouth in the morning be "two."
- Go to a restaurant and order the same entrée twice. Eat only one of the entrées, and think about how doubling the amount of food in front of you makes it possible to eat only half as much food. Cultivate a way to see all of your eating behavior as fundamentally illogical.
- Double other aspects of your life. For example, when you say thank you, say, "Thanks. Thanks a lot." See this chapter of your life as a time of doubling. Consider the fact that if you successfully

double everything in your life, you'll have only half the amount of time to accomplish anything. Recognize this as a way of achieving less by doing more. Be thankful for the "halvings" that may come from the "doublings."

- Consider doubling this directive: Use four forks instead of two, say four prayers instead of two, and so forth. Before trying this, ask yourself whether more is always better.

- As a radical change of pace, do the opposite: Cut a plastic spoon in half, along with a fork. Eat with half a utensil and half a prayer. Make a comparison study with your previous efforts.

## ✦ DIRECTIVE: SACRED VOID

Arrange your meals and your food on half of a plate. Keep the other side empty. Call this other side a "sacred void." Stare at the void when eating your meal. Do this whenever you feel your eating habits need a spiritual infusion.

### Considerations

- Consider other ways to bring emptiness into your life. For example, empty one drawer (or half a drawer) in your dresser, make an empty space in your refrigerator, keep an empty shoe box in your closet, and so forth.

- Write the words "empty void" on one palm. Make sure you look at it several times a day and see how easy it is to hold nothing.

- Do an Internet search on the meaning of the word *void*. Gain more knowledge about emptiness.

- Send a blank card to yourself, and then return a thank-you note to yourself that says, "Thanks for reminding me of nothing."

- As you stare at all the forms of emptiness that you've created in your life, think about wealth as the accumulation of less and less.

## ✦ DIRECTIVE: RESTRICTED ZONES

Draw an imaginary line dividing your kitchen in half. (You may use masking tape to create the line if you like.) Choose one side in which certain "problem" foods will be prohibited. Never eat a problem food in the prohibited zone. When struggling with an eating decision, place one foot on each side of the boundary line. Then decide.

## Considerations

- Draw lines, real and imaginary, to create boundaries in your life. For example, demarcate a zone in your office that is the only place you can utter certain words.
- Carry a piece of string. From time to time, pull it out and stretch it into a straight line. Consider how you can impose boundaries wherever you want them.
- Whenever you are tempted by anything and need to draw a boundary, get a pen and draw twenty-five lines on a small piece of paper.
- When you straddle a boundary, try leaning first to one side and then to the other. Rock or sway back and forth. See this as a way of simultaneously maintaining and erasing a boundary.
- Consider the Zen meaning of "not one, not two" while swaying back and forth across a boundary.

## ✦ Directive: Finger Bowl

Before a meal, fill a small bowl with warm water. Say a prayer to bless the water and place the bowl next to your plate. When you eat, place your smallest finger in the bowl of blessed water. Now eat with the other hand. Think about the blessed water and ask it to sanctify your eating habits.

## Considerations

- Do this with a different finger. Which finger is most sensitive to the exercise?
- Consider placing a toe or a whole foot into the bowl of blessed water.
- Rather than place a finger into the bowl, dip a small cross before each bite. Consider this to be the strongest form of the practice.
- Halfway through your meal, pour some of the water onto the remaining food.

- At the end of your meal, pour the remaining water into an ice tray and freeze it. Fill a significant portion of your freezer with these holy diet cubes.

## ✦ DIRECTIVE: "GO AHEAD, SUCKER!"

Go through newspapers and magazines, cutting out photographs of famous people you detest. Choose people that you can easily become angry about. Ideally, each picture will depict a person smiling or gloating. Paste thirteen of these clippings on a large piece of cardboard.

With stencil letters, write the following on top of this mini-billboard: "Go ahead, sucker! Take another bite for us. We don't care about your spiritual well-being." When you're struggling with your diet, pull this mini-billboard out of your closet and place it so you can see it while you are eating.

### Considerations
- Think about the many ways your enemies can inspire you to act.
- Consider the famous prayer, "Lord, grant me a worthy enemy." Think about the kind of enemy that can advance your life and the kind that is merely an annoyance.
- When your enemies are able to move you to action, thank them and say, "I have taken a first step toward loving my enemies."
- Meditate on the difference between loving to hate your enemy and hating to love them.
- If you wake up in the middle of the night and find yourself worrying about something over which you have no control, get out a flashlight and shine it on your billboard. See how happy the people in the pictures look.

## ✦ DIRECTIVE: THE CHARITABLE DIET

For every week in which you lose weight, donate five dollars to a religious organization you agree with. For every week that you gain weight, donate five dollars to a religious, political, or social organization you disagree with. If you feel the need, write an accompanying letter telling them why you disagree with their practices and beliefs and that you are sending them money as a punishment for something you wish you hadn't done.

### Considerations

- Raise the stakes to a higher amount.
- Rather than send money, send food.
- Find other people to join you in this practice. Consider creating a club that raises money in this way.
- When sending money or food to an organization you dislike, consider the consequences your weight gain is having in the world.
- When you attain your desired weight, send a gift to an organization that promotes humor. See how easy or difficult it is to find such a group.

## CONCLUDING THOUGHTS

"Stop playing with your food!" That's what we were taught when we were children. Not surprisingly, eating subsequently became an overly serious matter. We grew up and learned how to inappropriately take the satisfaction of eating too seriously and thereby ate too much. Or we took our overeating too seriously and made it a bigger problem than it should be. The latter dynamic led many of us into a classic double bind: the more successful we are at depriving ourselves, the more likely we will fail the next time we show up at the dining table.

The Christian shaman returns to the wisdom of childhood and proclaims, "Start playing with your food (and your diet)!" Only the absurd stands a chance of getting at the illogical ways that we become slaves of hunger pangs that we feel when our bodies are not really hungry. Dieting is a powerful laboratory for the shaman. It enables you to tinker in many ways, particularly with the trickster strategies that contrary presence calls for. Playfully enter into the madness of weight control, diets, and eating habits. Let the shamanic trickster truths play with the candy bars, second helpings, and late-night snacks. Say hello and goodbye to the disturbing eating habits. It's "ciao" time for the shaman!

## 22

# SHAMANIC DIRECTIVES FOR ADDRESSING SADNESS

*Truly, truly, I say to you, that you will weep and lament,*
*but the world will rejoice; you will be sorrowful, but your*
*sorrow will be turned to joy. Whenever a woman is in tra-*
*vail she has sorrow, because her hour has come; but when*
*she gives birth to the child, she remembers the anguish no*
*more, for joy that a child has been born into the world.*
*Therefore you too now have sorrow; but I will see you*
*again, and your heart will rejoice, and no one takes your*
*joy away from you.*

JOHN 16:20–22

## SHAMANIC LESSON

It is natural to feel sad sometimes. Sadness is a cleanser, a clearing, a healthy rain needed in every emotional climate. However, sometimes we can get overly concerned about these episodes of clouds and rain. The concern of others may cause us to worry even more about whether something is really wrong with us. That is the climatic condition that turns natural sadness into what some call depression.

Rejoice in the rains and immobility of sadness. See it as part of the larger cycles. But be careful when the snake of sadness feeds upon itself, resulting in a stuck or escalating sadness that feels like emotional quicksand. When that starts to happen, call in the tricksters. Introduce your sadness to the absurd players and let some ridiculous behavior ensue. Stretch any stuck sadness into a new shamanic dichotomy, with serious concern on one side and absurd play on the other side. Stretch it so fresh energy comes into your life. In this newly outstretched arm of the cross, transformation becomes possible.

## ✦ DIRECTIVE: WEEPING TONIC

Turn on your stereo and play the saddest spiritual music you can find. You may have to purchase a new recording to assure that you have some sad sounds. When the music is on, go to a faucet within hearing distance, and get it to drip as slowly as possible. Collect these drips in a glass. As you watch each drip, imagine that this is the Earth weeping. This water represents the Earth crying for all the sadness it feels from people who don't know what to do with their sadness.

When the glass is full, stop the music. Immediately turn on some ecstatic gospel music. As you listen to it, slowly drink the Earth's tears. Stretch out your drinking of the sacred water to last as long as the song lasts. See this drink as a healing tonic, medicine for your soul.

### Considerations

- Click your tongue to make a dripping sound. Make this sound occasionally throughout the day while you are working on this directive.
- One evening, make every faucet in your house drip. Do this for no longer than five minutes as you play the sad spiritual music. Send a postcard to a friend to tell them that every faucet in your house dripped for five minutes last night. Make certain that you write the card while listening to ecstatic gospel music.
- Make one sad sound and collect one drop of water onto the palm of your hand. Then make one wild happy sound and lick the moisture off your hand. Consider doing this at a public drinking fountain.

- Rather than drinking the healing tonic water, consider watering your plants with it.

## ✦ DIRECTIVE: MOSES AND THE PARTING OF THE WATERS

Think about the fact that your body is composed mostly of water. Give yourself five minutes to pause and think about this, allowing no other thought to enter your mind (as much as possible). Go to a stove and boil some water. When you see the steam float into the air, get an ice cube from your freezer. Hold this ice cube in one hand. In the other hand, hold a glass of water. Now drink the water while waving the ice near the steam. Be careful to not burn the hand holding the ice. Visualize Moses and how he was able to part the waters.

### Considerations

- Part a section of your hair with a comb after performing this practice and say, "Thank you, Moses."
- Patiently observe an ice cube melting. Consider this a meditation on Moses.
- Look up the weather reports from different cities. Find a city where it is raining, another city where there is fog, and another city where there is an ice storm. Write down the first day in which you find these conditions in three cities. Call it the Day of Moses.
- Find photos of water as liquid, steam, and ice. Attach them to your bathroom mirror. Look at each image when you comb your hair. Keep your mind on Moses as you look at the different forms of water.

## ✦ DIRECTIVE: SPIRITUAL LEVITATION

Consider what might be the opposite of depression. Depression often leaves one feeling unmotivated to get up and do much of anything. One may feel heavy, like absolute concrete. Seen this way, the opposite of depression could be levitation, the feeling of being so light you have springs in your feet—that with a little effort, you might even be tempted to believe you can fly.

One might think of depression, then, as a kind of "spiritual aeronautical problem." You've forgotten how to get any spiritual lift. The shamanic tonic you need requires recruiting four other people to stand around you as you sit in a chair. They will place their hands on top of your head in a stack of alternating hands. For three seconds, they will gently pump their hands up and down, saying, "Let's lift you up." On the count of three, they will attempt to lift your body with their fingers held under your knees, hips, and arms. The outcome will be astonishing. You will feel a defiance of gravity as your friends lift you into the air.

Your assignment is to have this "flight crew" available to you once a week. When you meet, you are to experience at least three "flights." In these moments of levity, allow your inner spirit to be fully shocked by the surprise of becoming airborne.

## Considerations

- Wear some airline wings when you become proficient with this exercise.
- Find out whether Houdini did this same levitation experiment.
- Have a party for your flight crew. Set records for lift-off height.
- Consider how this practice could change the world.
- Have another friend take photographs of your spiritual flights, and use these to make a photo album.

## ✦ DIRECTIVE: HUMOR BEAR

Go to a very large toy store and look for the saddest-looking teddy bear you can find. Purchase this companion and speak these words to it over and over on the way home: "I understand."

For the next week, ask everyone you know to give you a favorite joke. Tell them you are creating a collection of jokes. Write each joke on a tiny piece of colored paper. When you've collected at least fifty jokes, carefully open up the back end of your stuffed creature and push these jokes into it. You may have to reseal the creature's bottom with a safety pin.

Find a new joke every day. You may consult the library for joke books and you may call people on the phone to ask if they know any good jokes. It doesn't matter how you get the jokes. At the end of each day, place the new joke inside the bear. Over time you will have to remove the original stuffing of the bear until your bear is completely full of jokes.

When the bear is stuffed with jokes and it is impossible to feed another one into it, do the following. Keep the bear near you. When you see someone who complains about being sad, bring out the bear and pull out one joke. Tell them it is a form of community service you practice. You and your bear are responsible for seeding humor throughout the "sadlands" of contemporary society.

## Considerations

- Make some more humor bears as presents for others.
- Draw your humor bear on a small piece of paper and tape it to the back of your driver's license. Consider this your official license to spread humor across the land.
- Have someone make a video of you in action with your humor bear. Watch it once at three o'clock in the morning. Allow yourself to take one joke out of the bear after you have done this.
- Collect pictures of bears. Write jokes on the back of the pictures. Bring them to your humor bear so he or she does not become lonely.
- Go to a zoo and find a bear. Tell the bear one of your jokes.

## ✦ DIRECTIVE: SILLY CRITTERS

Look through some old magazines and cut out the saddest faces you can find. Create a small collection of these sad faces and set them aside. When this is done, hunt through the magazines for photos of cattle, horses, goats, chickens, and other familiar farm animals. Create a collection of these critters.

With these photos, you will create a children's book about spirituality. The book will be about animals with human sad faces. Paste the human faces onto the various animal bodies and line them up so you can see your cast of characters. Create a story by following this procedure:

1. Pick a character from one of your photo composites. Write a silly caption under it.
2. Create four more captions in this way.
3. Now arrange these captioned photo composites in some ordered sequence. Do your best to arrange them so that they create some kind of logical order.
4. Fill in the gaps between these captions with words to create a cohesive story with a beginning, middle, and end.
5. Attach the photos, captions, and story to the pages of a scrapbook so that you have a book. Give the book a title.
6. Go to a public library and leave this book on the shelf where self-help spirituality books are kept.

## Considerations

- Give yourself a pseudonym (a pen name) and sign the book with it.
- Consider making these books as gifts to adults.
- Choose the image and caption you are most proud of and have it framed. Hang it in your home.
- Do the directive in the opposite way: Find images of sad people and cut out their bodies. Now place animal head images on them and proceed with your captions and story.
- Experiment with using plant and flower images as faces or bodies. What difference does the plant kingdom bring to the exercise?

## ✦ DIRECTIVE: HUMOR INVASION

This task requires one full day and is best done with a friend or carload of friends. Get out your state map and choose three small towns that are near one another. They must be towns you have never visited. Drive to each town and get a feel for the town. You and your friends are to judge which town seems to be the saddest town. You will first have to decide what criteria you will use to determine the town's sadness. Will you make a judgment according to whether the buildings create an atmosphere of sadness? Or perhaps you will examine how the people look in each town. It's up to you and your friends to make the rules for this contest.

When you've decided which is the saddest town, do the following. Bring with you some copies of cartoons. (Past issues of *The New Yorker* magazine provide a rich source of delightful cartoons.) Distribute your cartoons throughout the town. Make sure that you say, "St. Basil blesses you with holy foolishness" for each cartoon that you place in the town. Put them in a variety of different places: perhaps in the local churches, in a few diners, on a gas pump, even on the town statue. It's up to you to determine how you'll "invade" the winning town.

## Considerations

- Consider using other sources of cartoons, or find someone who can draw and make cartoons specific to the town.
- Find out everything you can about St. Basil. You may want to sign each cartoon with his name.
- Always keep a couple of cartoons with you, so you are prepared to leave them in a place that looks as if it needs a boost.
- Make a pledge to deposit at least three cartoons each week at a place of your choice.

## ✦ DIRECTIVE: ENDANGERED SPECIES

Imagine being an animal that is a sad member of an endangered species. Write a prayer for the human race as if you were this animal and had been given a chance to say anything you want. Sign the prayer with the animal's name. Send this prayer to someone you believe would be touched by this gesture.

## Considerations

- Send these prayers to churches and temples and other holy places. Ask them to read it to their congregations.
- Send a prayer to your local newspaper.
- Place this prayer next to you when you sleep. If you dream of the animal, make that animal your personal cause and mail its prayer to at least one hundred people or organizations.

- Make a prayer for the animal after reading its prayer.
- Have an artist make the prayer into a creative and beautiful presentation for your home.

## ✦ DIRECTIVE: ONE DROP AT A TIME

The next time you are sad and can't release your sadness, try the following. Draw the outline of a one-inch-high teardrop on a piece of paper and cut it out. Make seven of these paper teardrops. On each drop write out what you are sad about. At the end of your description write this sentence, "It is now time to_____." Open the dictionary to any page and place your finger on a word at random. That is the word your sentence will end with.

You are to work with these drops for seven days. Carry a drop with you each day until you find just the right spot in which to leave it. Do not release more than one drop per day. Over the next week, you will continue to drop one tear each day in a place of your choice. Make a silent prayer for each teardrop, asking that it make a difference in someone's life. See yourself as watering the barren souls of the world.

### Considerations

- Consider attaching strings to your drops and hanging them at the chosen spots.
- Hang a drop over your bed and let it sleep above you the night before you put it into the world.
- Place your drop in a glass of water. Dry it and then release it into the world.
- Make a foot-long drop and mail it to a politician. Send other drops to local news reporters.
- Hang one drop beneath a faucet in your home. Think of this as an empowerment of the practice.

## ✦ DIRECTIVE: MYSTERY LETTERS

Take a sheet of paper and cut out the letter *s*. The letter should be the size of the original paper with enough room inside its border to write a letter on. Write a letter on it to someone whose name begins with an *s*. Mail them the letter.

A week later, cut out the letter *a*. This time write and mail a letter to a person whose name begins with *a*. The following week, prepare a *d*, write a letter to a person with a *d* name, and mail that.

Should any of your letter recipients ask you why you chose to write a letter on a letter, send them this letter in reply:

> Dear Friend,
>
> Thank you for asking about the significance of the letter. It is part of a mystery I'm still trying to figure out. All I can tell you is that I was told to use letters as a means of sending letters. Do you want to know more?

If they ask again for the meaning, send them a copy of this book and tell them they must read every word to insure that they understand the letter. If they do so, you know they will be reading these words when they get to this point in the book:

> Dear Participant,
>
> Thank you for participating in this assignment. Your reading of these very words insures that the task has moved along in the way it was designed to. It is important that you now know that you are to supply the meaning of the letter. You are to create this meaning in the following way:

1. Send a letter to three people you know who you believe are spiritually creative and inventive. Ask them to answer this question: "I received a letter that was written on an s (or a or d). What do you think this could mean? I'm looking for spiritual answers. Could you send me your interpretations of this mystery?"

2. Collect all the answers you get and mail them to the person who first sent you the letter. Ask him or her to select the answer or meaning they like best and inform you by letter.

3. Send the results to everyone who supplied you with spiritual answers.

## Considerations

- Place an *s* in one room of your house, an *a* in another room, and a *d* in a different room. Write the names of the people to whom you sent letters on the letters that correspond to their names. Pray for them every time you walk near the letter.
- Place an *s* on your front bumper and an *a* and a *d* on the back bumper. Wait for someone to ask what this means and then invite them to join your search for spiritual answers.
- Make a mobile to hang in your room out of the three letters, *s, a,* and *d.* If you eventually receive spiritual answers from your original letter recipients, write your collected spiritual answers on them.
- Decide which letter brought you the best answers. Make it your spiritual letter. Make a small altar for it.
- Determine which letter brought you the least interesting answers. Make a prayer for the letter and ask that it be given deeper meanings. Send it out to other people with the hope that the letter will be empowered spiritually by your prayers and steadfastness.

## CONCLUDING THOUGHTS

The sacred clowns and tricksters of other cultures set no limits on how they enact the contraries of life. At a joyous situation they will cry and at a sad situation they will laugh. In the stretching of those contraries, greater truths and possibilities for transformation are more likely to enter the scene. Similarly, the Christian shaman respectfully disrespects solemn and serious occasions, including the manifestation of sadness. Popular culture sings, "Don't worry, be happy. Don't be sad, be happy." This is often ineffective because saying no to that which is present may paradoxically strengthen its presence. The shaman says, "Worry and thereby become happy. Be sad and thereby become happy." The way out is through getting further in, playing, and setting the stage for transformation. Don't be sad about your sadness. Be happy about it and play with it. Yes, at first, you will still be sad, but you will be happy with how you are with your sadness. This, in turn, creates an opening for anything to take place, including a spiritual giggle followed by an earthy belly laugh.

# 23

# SHAMANIC DIRECTIVES
# fOR ADDRESSING
# BOREDOM

*Remember the sabbath day, to keep it holy. Six days shalt
thou labour, and do all thy work: But the seventh day is
the sabbath of the LORD thy God: in it thou shalt not
do any work, thou, nor thy son, nor thy daughter, thy
manservant, nor thy maidservant, nor thy cattle, nor
thy stranger that is within thy gates: For in six days the
LORD made heaven and earth, the sea, and all that in
them is, and rested the seventh day: wherefore the LORD
blessed the sabbath day, and hallowed it.*

EXODUS 20:8–11

## SHAMANIC TEACHING

It is important to take time to do nothing, and even more important to
become bored from time to time. Think of boredom and doing nothing
as a necessary process of composting for action yet to come. Christian
shamans know what to do with boredom. They embrace it, play with it,
and stretch it with absurd directives. Shamans wait patiently until boredom shows up in their lives. Then they catch it and make it an object of
teasing and trickster experiments. Boredom is easy to mess with. Doing

*anything* with boredom is better than being bored with boredom. Learn to be interested with the boredom that comes into your life. See it as an opportunity for radical play.

## ✦ DIRECTIVE: MAKING THE UNINTERESTING INTERESTINGLY UNINTERESTING

Think of an inexpensive religious product that does not interest you. Take a friend or family member to the store where this product is sold and try to convince this person that you're very interested in it. After a suitable period of time, tell your friend you're not going to buy it. Explain that, among other things, you are practicing saying "no" to spiritual things you don't really need.

### *Considerations*

- What makes some religious items uninteresting? Write down your answer and leave it near the item at the store.
- Make a list of your top ten uninteresting religious items or symbols. Using your imagination, make the list interesting.
- Make an interesting "no" by drawing it, sculpting it, or symbolizing it in any way you see fit. Mail it to an uninteresting object. For example, mail it to "The Boring Picture on aisle 3, shelf 2, Christian Religious Supplies, 1200 Thomas Street, Anytown, Anystate."
- Think of something uninteresting about an interesting religious object, and something interesting about an uninteresting object.
- Place an interesting religious article in the least interesting place in your house. Notice whether the spot becomes more interesting, whether the object becomes less interesting, or both.

## ✦ DIRECTIVE: THE RITUAL OF REVERSAL

When you are absolutely stuck in the quicksand of boredom, perform the following shamanic ritual:

1. Lie down on your bed the wrong way, with you head resting on the end of the bed and your feet on the pillow. Do this for one minute.
2. Slide out of the bed and lie on the floor. Do not stand up.
3. Crawl to your front door.
4. Walk around the outside of your home or apartment, keeping your head turned to the right.
5. Walk the opposite way around your home or apartment with your head turned to the left.
6. Reenter your front door.
7. Crawl backward to your bed.
8. Lie down on your bed and be still for one minute.
9. Say "Amen." Then say "Awomen."
10. Sit up and think about how three of your friends would react if they watched a videotape of what you just did.
11. See if you can persuade a friend to do this ritual with you. Make a date to perform it.

## Considerations

- Select the part of this ritual that was strangest for you to perform. For a week, do only this part of the ritual once a day. See if the task becomes stranger or less strange with practice.
- Eliminate three parts of the ritual. Consider this a fine-tuning.
- Choose one part of the ritual that you will repeat twice.
- Experiment with the order of the actions.
- Predict what your friend will choose regarding the above considerations. Try out what they choose. Do you like their choices better than yours?

## ✦ DIRECTIVE: MIXED-UP READINGS

Read the first half of the first chapter of any spiritual book. Read the second half of the first chapter of another spiritual book. Next, go to the library and read only the last pages of several spiritual books you believe you will probably never read.

Tell someone about a book you wish you could write based on the information you gathered in the previous reading assignments. You can make up or add whatever you need for the story to make sense. Keep trying to tell the story to different people until you believe you have developed an interesting spiritual teaching.

## Considerations

- Try reading the first half of the first chapter of a spiritual book, followed by the second half of the first chapter of a book that has nothing to do with spirituality. Add randomly selected sentences from randomly selected books. Mix them up and then try to make the story make sense.
- Take three sentences from any three books and string them together. Consider it a riddle for a Christian shaman to ponder.
- Ask other people to each send you a sentence from one of their favorite books. Combine these to create a spiritual teaching.
- Start collecting sentences that make no sense from books. Write these sentences down and carry them with you. Meditate on them, and wait for interesting meanings and connections and insights to emerge. On one day of the week, pretend this is an extremely important exercise. On the very next day, pretend it is utter nonsense. Continue alternating your belief about this work.

## ✦ Directive: Bedroom Labyrinth

Take a photograph of your left shoe, then take a photograph of your right shoe. Go to a copy shop and make twenty-five copies of each photograph.

Pin up or tape these copies on your bedroom wall, as if an invisible person wearing your shoes were walking up the wall. Continue putting up these footprints so they travel all the way around your room—up one wall, across the ceiling, down the other wall, across the floor, and round and round again.

When you finish walking around your room, sit in the middle of the room and stare at the footprints. Fantasize about what it would be like to actually be able to walk this way.

Show these footprints to your friends and tell them you are inventing a new form of shamanic practice. Call it the bedroom labyrinth. If you find someone who expresses a genuine interest in what you have done, ask if you can photograph their shoes too. Repeat the procedure and add their footprints to your room.

## Considerations

- When you have placed another person's steps in your room, imagine walking in their shoes and wait to see how long it takes for you to gain a new understanding of this person.
- Change from shoe images to hand prints. Imagine walking around your room on your hands.
- Draw yellow lines on pieces of paper so as to make a road on your wall. Imagine traveling on it in a tiny vehicle.
- Place strings all around your room. Imagine gliding along those strings.
- Take a photograph of your room and carry it with you. Continue your imaginary journeys in other places.

## ✦ DIRECTIVE: POSTCARD NONSENSE

Purchase ten postcards. On each card, write a sentence of nonsense. You may make up your own nonsense or choose from the following selections:

"It's time to invert the sound that slaps our saint."
"May your day fall over the hole behind the heavens."
"What isn't known can't be blamed for the four-cornered cross."
"Yellow is the shape of my friend's best prayer."
"I met a blade of grass that kicked a vision right between your career."
"Now is the past her future forgot to forgive."
"'What' is the name of a retired 'why.'"
"Never allow an ever to stammer your taste for wonder."
"If you read that, this will submerge into the face of the spiritually absent."

"There will always be a b in the buzz of a silent bee."

"Have a day that has forgotten its place in the dreams of lesser gods."

"Today is the beginning of all that won't allow the great will of thrill."

"How do you throw an expectation into the machines that bark?"

"I love eating nonsense sentences on behalf of your neighbor's best garden."

"Do you find the smell of sense in the unscented sense of sensible nonsense?"

"This is the end of what began before all else ended our other beginnings."

Mail these postcards of nonsense to your friends. Make sure each card is signed, "Christian Shaman-in-Training." Wonder about what your friends will wonder about when they look at your card.

## Considerations

- Consider why you haven't sent nonsense before.
- Say a nonsense prayer.
- Make a nonsense pledge to your partner.
- Prepare a nonsense meal.
- Go on a nonsense weekend getaway.

✦ DIRECTIVE: KINGDOM OF BOREDOM

On a small piece of paper write the letters *b-o-r-e*. On another piece of paper write the letters *d-o-m*. Place these pieces of paper in front of you on a table surface and place one thumb on each piece. Move your thumbs in a circular pattern, swirling the pieces of paper around. As you do this, read the following statement aloud as loudly as you can:

*The kingdom of boredom is ruled by a bore. The bore is not a dumb bore, but a king without a holy boar.*

Repeat this ritual once an evening throughout the next week. The next week, you are to gather as many photographs or drawings of hogs (or boars) as you can, making as large a collection as possible. You will need at least twenty-five pictures. When you have finished making your collection, sit down again with your pieces of paper—the *b-o-r-e* and the *d-o-m*. Swirl them with your thumbs and say:

> *Now the king has some boar. The king wasn't really a bore, nor was the boar a bore. It's the kingdom that's troubled, for it's not yet part of the spiritual lore.*

Purchase a map of the world and select a spot in which to locate this imaginary kingdom. Hang the map on your wall and place a colored pin or flag marker on the spot you choose. On that spot, write the name of the kingdom, *Boredom*.

## Considerations
- Consider whether heaven has bores.
- How might heaven be boring if, in fact, it is boring? What could you do to make it less boring, should the opportunity present itself?
- Make up other imaginary kingdoms and mark them on your map.
- Imagine that God has allowed you to create seven different heavens. What would they be? Name them and mark them on your map.
- Imagine that heaven allows its members to take a vacation every once in a while. Where would you go? Make sure this place is circled on the map and labeled "vacation from heaven."

## ✦ DIRECTIVE: PRAYING WITH A BORING BOOK

Go to your local public library and randomly walk through the book stacks. Without thinking or looking at what you're choosing, select ten books from different places in the library. Sit down with these books and, without looking at a single page, choose the book you believe will be the most boring. Check it out and take it to your home.

Place this book that you assume is boring on top of your television so it is clearly visible. Before you turn on the television, open the book and immediately say, "Dear Lord." Read one sentence aloud, then say, "Amen." Perform this ritual every time you do anything with the television set. If you turn it off, change the channel, or adjust the volume, you must say, "Dear Lord," read a sentence aloud, and end with "Amen."

Do this for two weeks. At the end of this time, write a letter to the author of the book. Tell the author what you did with the book and describe any interesting experiences you had as a result of this task. Enclose the letter in the middle of the book and return it to the library.

## Considerations

- Consider boredom as compost that is necessary to fertilize the more interesting experiences.
- Plan a way to be bored that you haven't experienced before.
- Do you find the word "boredom" boring? What letter could you add to the word to make it more interesting?
- Who is the most bored person you know? Who is the least bored? How would they get along? Might one influence the other? Consider arranging a party to which both are invited.
- Choose one day of the month (or half a day) that you devote to being bored.

## ✦ Directive: Weird Spiritual Calls

Select any or all of the following phone tasks to carry out:

1. Call a pet store and ask if they sell biblical whales.
2. Call a drugstore and ask if they sell holy water.
3. Call a university's department of religion and ask if they have any spiritual visions.
4. Call a library and ask if they will read a Bible verse to you over the phone.

5. Call the manager of a religious bookstore and ask if they have any books on Christian shamanism.

6. Call a church and ask if God will be attending their next service.

7. Call a funeral home and ask if they have ever seen a ghost.

8. Call a music store and ask the person who answers to tell you his or her favorite spiritual chord.

9. Call a bank and ask if they give any money away to the poor.

10. Call a telephone operator and ask whether he or she believes people are becoming more or less spiritual on the phone these days.

11. Call someone in your family and explain about all these phone calls.

12. Call a friend and tell him or her about your conversation with your family member.

13. Call a newspaper and ask to whom you should submit a story about your calls.

## Considerations

- Write down all of the phone numbers you called in this exercise. Place them inside your Bible for twenty-four hours and then decide what needs to be done with them. Pray for direction.

- Write down the three most interesting responses you received. Write them in your Bible as if they were newly discovered verses.

- Write down the name of the person or place from which you received the least interesting answer. Make a special prayer for this person or place and call them again in a year.

- How do you think each person would have responded if they believed you were an agent of God?

- How do you think you would respond if you received these calls? Write down your responses to each of the questions.

✦ DIRECTIVE: BOREDOM SURVEY

Make your own spiritual survey on boredom. Create a list of at least ten questions about boredom. Do not ask normal questions, such as what makes people get bored, how often they get bored, what they do about it, and so forth. Instead, explain that you are conducting a spiritual investigation of boredom and ask unusual questions, such as the following:

1. Do you know the historical origin of the word "boredom?"
2. If you were never bored, would you get bored with never getting bored?
3. What time during the night is the least boring?
4. I'm trying to get more boredom in my life. Do you have any suggestions?
5. Do you think anyone ever taught a course on boredom?
6. Are there therapists who specialize in treating boredom?
7. What is the most boring word in the English language?
8. Show me how you look when you get bored.

## Considerations

- Could this kind of research lead you to becoming an interesting authority on the subject of boredom?
- What was your most boring question on boredom? The most interesting?
- Find three people who are fluent in another language. Have them teach you a foreign word for boredom. Chose the foreign word that sounds the most interesting. Stop using the English word "boredom" and instead use the foreign word you have chosen.
- Invent an alternative word for boredom, like "yaaadoo." Think of this word when you feel bored.
- What color is most boring to you? Go to a hardware store and get a paint sample card of that color. Carry it with you. Leave it at the next boring situation you are in.

## ✦ Directive: The World's Most Boring Ritual

With a group of shamanically oriented friends, try to perform the world's most boring ritual. Plan and create the most boring feast, the most boring icons and decorations, the most boring attire, the most boring music, and the most boring things to say and do.

Hire someone to videotape the ritual. All of you must keep in mind that if someone is seen having fun, laughing, or smiling, the ritual is failing. You may have to have designated individuals who patrol the ritual on the lookout for anyone who isn't bored. Anyone who is not bored may have to go to a penalty area for a few minutes. Remember this must be *the most boring* ritual ever experienced on planet Earth.

### Considerations

- Send out an invitation that begins, "You are invited to the world's most boring ritual . . ."
- Ask people for advice on how to make the ritual boring.
- Write dictionary definitions of *boredom* on the napkins.
- Make this an annual event. Perhaps perform it on the holiday you all find most boring.
- Consider making boring masks for people to wear.

## CONCLUDING THOUGHTS

When you're bored, do something really different (but be smart and don't get into serious trouble). Boredom is an invitation to stretch your self into a new space. It is a calling to be creative with your stuck situation. Nothing's happening when you're bored so no time will be wasted if you try a little experimentation. Appreciate boredom as a time out to tinker with yourself and the situations you are in. Say thank you to your times of boredom. Imagine that they are a vacation from predictable behavior. They free you to improvise with imagination. Go ahead, get bored and let the trickster run free. Boredom is the ding-a-ling-a-ling for the trickster within you to wake up and stir things up. Become a Jesus coyote. Pray an odd prayer, make up a weird hymn, and dance down an imaginary church aisle with a very strange movement whenever boredom throws a party.

# 24

# SHAMANIC DIRECTIVES
# FOR ADDRESSING ANGER

*Be ye angry, and sin not: let not the sun go down upon your wrath.*

EPHESIANS 4:26

## SHAMANIC TEACHING

Anger is another way energy is brought to us to sustain life. But anger is also wrath that can harm yourself and others. When anger strikes, go after the energy, but stretch yourself away from the wrath. Here you must allow the absurd to step in quickly, utilize the energy to immediately act, and stretch anger into the dimension of play. It is often difficult to pull yourself away from the throes of anger. It may help to carry a tiny bell with you. Ring it when you feel the anger beginning to escalate. Focus on hearing the sound and do your best to step aside and give yourself a time out, allowing you to complete a shamanic directive.

When one can stretch anger between the ends of serious upset and ridiculous madness, a very strong spiritual arm of the cross can be created. Loving one's enemy is the strongest medicine, the most powerful shamanic ritual, and the most transformative shape-shift. Accept anger as one of the greatest gifts you can receive. It's powerful, like nitroglycerine, but when handled appropriately, can blow your mind open to new shamanic dimensions.

## ✦ DIRECTIVE: "ANGUH" BOX

Obtain a medium-sized cardboard box and place some plastic fruit inside it. Print these words on the outside of the box:

> He who is slow to anger, is better than the mighty, and he who rules his spirit, better than he who captures a city.

When you feel that your anger is about to get out of control, go to the box and open its top. Open your mouth as wide as you can, but do not make a sound. Bend over with your head over the box's opening and imagine the excess anger pouring out of your mouth. In your mind's eye, imagine it as a vaporous gas.

Allow enough time to fully empty this vapor of anger into the container. Close the top and wait patiently for one minute as you imagine the vapor being stabilized and neutralized by the sweetness of the fruit. At the end of this time, open the lid, light a match, and hold it in the middle of the box. This will show you that the vapor is no longer volatile.

### Considerations

- Experiment with making a monkey or gorilla sound when you open your mouth.
- Imagine that the vapor does explode, but in another dimension.
- Place a real fruit alongside the plastic fruit. See if this makes the exercise more real for you.
- If possible, keep the anger box near a fire extinguisher.
- For the scripture written on the box, spell *anger* as "anguh." Think about how this change of spelling might alter your understanding and/or experience of anger.

## ✦ DIRECTIVE: THE FALLEN FINGER

Choose one finger that you will designate "the fallen finger—the finger of anger." Whenever you are angry, flutter this finger in a rapid vibratory movement. Imagine that its vibration is the energy pulse of your anger. Keep vibrating that angry finger until you sense that your anger is starting to feel tired.

### Considerations

- Consider drawing two horns on the fingernail of the fallen finger.
- Call the fallen finger "a bedeviled digit."
- Write a thank-you letter to your bedeviled digit, thanking it for volunteering for a necessary job.
- Try to see anger simply as energy gone astray. Think of how the wind and water and sun can be dangerous, but can also be harnessed and converted into practical energy. Imagine how your fluttering finger of anger might be harnessed—perhaps by scratching a part of your body that has an itch.
- Let another finger take over the job from time to time. The duty should be passed around.

### ✦ DIRECTIVE: THE CHARGED CARD

Choose a person you think may have been the angriest person in the history of the world. On a stiff piece of cardboard the size of a credit card, write this angry person's name. On the other side, write these words:

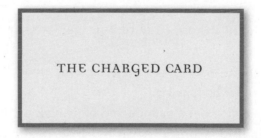

THE CHARGED CARD

Carry this anger card in your wallet. When you feel an angry voice speaking through you, open your wallet, pull out your anger card, and look at the name printed on it. With a shamanic attitude, imagine squeezing your anger into this card. Say, "With the help of three saints, help me put my anger into this card." After vigorously doing this, turn the card over to the other side and read the words you wrote there earlier.

## Considerations

- When you see someone else getting angry, squeeze your charged card. See this as a means of keeping your card calibrated and ready for future action.
- If the card gets too hot (overcharged), cool it off with an ice cube.
- Write an expiration date on the card. Make sure you renew it in the future.
- Write down the names of three of the angriest people who ever lived. Combine their names into one name by mixing up the letters. Turn this into a supercharged card.

## ✦ DIRECTIVE: SPIRITUAL ADJUSTMENTS

The next time you feel so angry that you begin worrying about your ability to control your temper, sit down and take off your right shoe. Reach over and squeeze your big toe ten times and tap your heel three times. With your index finger poke the middle part of your foot and hold it there for five seconds. Say silently, "Release it, Lord." If anyone asks what you are doing tell them you have an old injury that sometimes heats up, requiring you to make an adjustment.

## Considerations

- After saying "Release it, Lord," imagine a sacred wind cooling things off.
- Try variations of this exercise using your elbow, shoulder blade, knee, or other body parts.
- Consider taking out a balloon and blowing it up. If someone asks what you're doing, say it's an old Irish treatment for spiritual asthma.
- Take out a balloon and write the word *air* on it at least twelve times. As you are writing, tell yourself that you are filling it up with a different kind of air.
- Think of anger as a reminder to adjust your whole being, something that needs to be done on a regular basis.

## ✦ DIRECTIVE: SHOCK TREATMENT

Wait for the next time you get in a heated argument with someone with whom you have a close relationship. As the argument escalates into anger, hand the other person a card the size of a business card that says:

Immediately say, "Excuse me. I had to do that." Offer no explanation other than, "I'm trying to develop a shamanic shock card. It may be connected to a lost book of the Bible. What do you think?"

### Considerations

- What other kinds of shamanic shock cards can you imagine? Might you simply print "Shamanic Shock Card"?
- Bring more shock into your life. Perhaps you can keep an unexpected message or image inside your shirt or blouse and reveal it at the appropriate moment. How about carrying beans in your pocket and giving them away at unexpected moments?
- Consider carrying a short electrical extension cord with you. Pull it out when it is time to shock yourself. Carry a receptacle you can plug it into. Pretend to get shocked.
- Under dry conditions, rub your feet against a carpet and shock yourself whenever you think it could do you some good. Consider it a benign form of spiritual lightning.
- When you need a shock, jump in the air or jerk your arm for a second, pretending that a miniature lightning bolt hit you. If anyone sees this, say, "Don't worry. I'm just practicing my spirituality." Don't say anything more. If necessary, explain that you haven't yet gotten to the part of the lesson that tells you how to explain the practice.

## ✦ DIRECTIVE: REDUCTIO AD ABSURDUM

Make a list of all the angry words you really don't ever want to say to anyone but feel tempted to say when you become extremely angry. Using an extrafine pen, write these words on a piece of paper.

Take the list of "no-no words" to a copy shop and reduce it to a smaller size. Keep making reduced copies until it is impossible to read what you wrote. Every time you reduce it, say, "Take it away, Lord."

Carry these angry words with you. The next time you're angry and tempted to launch some of these words, pull out your invisible list and pretend to read it.

### Considerations

- Make another list that presents no-no words in a different way. For example, write "bad word," "terrible word," "shouldn't-say word," "forbidden word," "horrible word," "nasty word," "really steamed word," and so forth. Take it to a copy shop and reduce it, the same way you did with the first list.
- Choose the worst word you can ever imagine saying. Now think of this word while writing down another word that is neutral. Whenever you get really angry, say this alternative, neutral word. Only you will know what it means.
- Select the least harmful word you can imagine. Pretend that it means something horrible in another language. Consider using it in a heated situation.
- Make a copy of your hand "flipping the bird." Now cut out the image of your middle finger and throw away the rest of the paper. Draw a picture of a bird on it. Keep this with you and pull it out when necessary to defuse a runaway argument.
- In private, cuss out a bad word. Imagine that the bad word is a person who needs a good cussing. After you finish, apologize to the word and say you will try to be gentle with it in the future.

### ✦ DIRECTIVE: WALKING ON WATER

When your anger boils in the home, place your elbow on an ice cube either on the floor or on a counter, and scoot the cube from one corner of the kitchen to another corner. Imagine that this is a shamanic way of walking on water.

## *Considerations*

- Go watch a television news program that you know will make you angry. Immediately fetch the ice cube and "walk on water."
- If you are in a restaurant and get angry, take a tiny piece of ice and scoot it across your edge of the table with your elbow. If anyone asks what you are doing, say, "It's a pain reliever. I have a touchy elbow."
- Select the piece of ice you will use beforehand and say a blessing over it. Keep it ready in the freezer.
- If you are experiencing too much anger in your life, empty most of your freezer and fill it with blessed ice.
- Consider other ways shamanic ice can be used in your life. For example, after a particularly challenging day, make yourself a nice cold drink with this ice. Think of it cooling down your whole being.

### ✦ DIRECTIVE: COOKING THE SCRIPTURE

Place at least three alarm clocks on a table in your house. Place nothing else on this table except a Bible that has been wrapped with aluminum foil. When an argument with a family member turns into heated anger, both of you are to go to the table and turn on every alarm. You may not speak a word, but are allowed to cover your ears. Endure this alarm for at least several minutes. Then, without uttering a sound, go to a closet and retrieve a package of red-hot candies you placed there in preparation for such an occasion. Each of you is to place one candy in the other's mouth. Try to take this task as seriously as you can. After you have each sucked on the red-hot candy for ten seconds, you may each say one word to the other person.

## *Considerations*

- Try unwrapping the Bible and opening it to one word. Speak that word aloud. Do not say anything else for thirty minutes. Make sure that the Bible is then wrapped back up in foil.
- View this exercise as a biblical barbecue. Use the heat of your argument to fire a spiritual oven. Pretend it prepares your Bible to yield a perfectly done word that is perfect for you.
- Imagine that the sound of the alarms is the sound you wish you could make. Think how more satisfying it would be to sound an alarm, rather than spew out words.
- Consider placing your foil-wrapped Bible in your oven as the alarms go off. (There's no need to turn on the oven.) Remove when the alarms are silent again.
- Place your wrapped Bible on some charcoals. You can even place a drop of hot sauce on the Bible as the alarms are sounding.

## ✦ DIRECTIVE: PRIZEFIGHT

When caught in the habit of arguing with your intimate other, stop and think of yourselves as two professional prizefighters. In the room where most of your word fights take place, put a stool in each corner, as in a professional boxing ring. Under each stool, place a water bottle with a mist attachment. A clean and folded towel and a pair of boxing shorts should rest on top of each stool.

Keep a bell in this room that you can ring whenever a heated argument breaks out. When the bell is rung, both of you must run to the room and, as quickly as you can, peel off your clothes and change into your boxer shorts. Spray some mist all over your body, particularly your face, and then stand facing one another. You are now to exchange puffs of air at one another for sixty seconds. You may not puff on the other's face, but can blow on any other part of their body. No spitting or words are allowed—only wind puffs. Ring the bell to signal the end of the round. Spray yourself and use a towel if necessary to dry off uncomfortable wetness. Do this until one of you says, "Isn't it strange that the Holy Spirit is a wind?"

## Considerations

- Meditate on why the Holy Spirit is a wind. Contemplate the value of creating a situation that requires wind. Learn to appreciate the many facets of your emotional being.
- Arrange for a time to be angry together. Pretend to be angry if you can't get angry. Do the exercise in this condition.
- Videotape the performance of this ritual. The next time you get angry at one another, immediately put on the videotape and watch it.
- Make sure you are angry enough to do the exercise. If you are angry and find yourself unwilling to do this exercise, then pretend to be even angrier so you will get more motivated to get on with your spiritual lesson.
- For practice, take on another couple's anger. Imagine that you are role-playing their lives and act it out, doing so in your boxing ring.

## ✦ DIRECTIVE: TEMPER MEMORIALS

The next time you feel like losing your temper, escape to a private place and write these words on the floor with a pencil:

### IN MEMORY OF MY TEMPER

Be sure to write the exact date underneath this memorial to your anger.

## Considerations

- Make a clay tombstone for your temper.
- Write an obituary for a hot-tempered moment.
- Send flowers for the death of another hot-tempered moment.
- Mail your temper a bereavement card. Address it to "Temper, c/o (your name)."
- As you tame your temper, start referring to it as "Tempy."

### ✦ DIRECTIVE: UNDER LOCK AND KEY

Purchase a lock and key from a hardware store. On the lock print the word *anger*. To the key, attach the word *control*. Carry this lock and key with you when you think you may be getting into a situation that may tempt your temper. When the temptation to let out a burst of anger strikes you, pull out the lock and unlock it with your key. Imagine your anger being released without your having to say a word. Wait a few minutes and then lock it up again. View this as a spiritual practice. Imagine other ways in which you might use keys to lock and unlock other challenges in your life.

### Considerations
- Fortify your lock and key by reading them a scripture.
- Sanctify your lock and key by baptizing them and making a prayer for their assistance in your life.
- After practicing for a while, see if you can get along with nothing but the key. Keep the lock at home in a safe place. Hold the anger until you get home, then lock it up.
- Paint the key red, so it is obvious that this is an anger key.
- As you get your temper under control, get a smaller lock and key.

### ✦ DIRECTIVE: ANGER CODE

When it's impossible to keep from spewing out your anger, do it in code. Instead of saying, "You *#*@&! How can you be such an #%*hole?" try saying, "You meteor! How did you leave such a big crater?"

Say this as if you were actually saying the curse words. Imagine you are saying the toxic words through a secret code or voice translator. You know what you are really saying, although others don't have a clue. Think about this way of talking as a long-forgotten technique of Christian shamanism.

## Considerations

- Imagine that the only words you ever say to others are "God loves you." Now proceed to talk as you normally do, but do so believing that all of your words are simply a translation of "God loves you."
- Pretend you have a puppet in your hand. Move your fingers and silently tell other people things you don't feel you can say aloud.
- Consider that a person's spirit guide is standing next to them. Send that guide assurance that you want the best for both of them. Do this by nodding from time to time.
- Silently ask the spirit guide how to get along with the other person.
- Ask the spirit guide to send a message to God, saying you are working together.

## ✦ DIRECTIVE: FINDING YOUR LOST TEMPER

The next time you're about to lose your temper with your spouse, say aloud, "I've lost my temper. I need to find it before my soul starts looking." Even if you blow it, as soon as you notice you've lost your temper stop and say, "Damn it! I lost my temper again." At this point, begin asking your spouse for clues about where she or he has hidden your temper. Your spouse will have previously hidden an envelope labeled with the word "temper." The envelope will contain a description of the prize you get for finding your temper. This prize should be something that brings pleasure and surprise to both of you.

## Considerations

- Practice this when you're not angry. See it as preparation for the real thing.
- Rather than writing the word "temper" on an envelope, choose a toy animal to represent your temper. Have your spouse hide the critter. If you can't find a toy animal, then use a hot chile pepper or a bottle of hot sauce.
- Give your temper a phone number. Call the number when your temper is lost.

- Build an altar that honors your temper. It is part of you, so honor it and make clear that it is under spiritual management.

## CONCLUDING THOUGHTS

We're taught that anger is a tough challenge. It is supposed to be nearly impossible to control and when it gets ignited, look out because we are not supposed to be able to stop it in midcourse. The Christian shaman knows better. If you were in the heat of anger and an Unidentified Flying Object flew in front of you, believe me, you would instantly forget about being angry. Similarly, if an erotic stimulus suddenly came upon you, anger would disappear faster than a speeding bullet. Anger doesn't discourage the Christian shaman. Its appearance as a tough Brutus is simply seen as a masquerade. Anger's outer face may appear unchangeable, but on the inside it is a shamanic pussycat.

With the spirit of contrary trickster wisdom, practice seeing anger as a pushover. Believe that it can be stilled at a second's notice. Visualize yourself doing this. See if you can make it happen once. Simulate an angry moment and immediately perform its transformation. If you can alter anger and take it to absurd places, you will be well on your way to shamanic mastery.

# 25

# SHAMANIC DIRECTIVES
# FOR ADDRESSING FAMILY
# RELATIONSHIPS

*Honor thy father and thy mother, that thy days may be
long upon the land which the Lord thy God giveth thee.*

EXODUS 20:12

## SHAMANIC TEACHING

As it is wise to honor all that life brings to you, whether packaged as joy
or suffering, honor thy parents. Furthermore, it is wise to view what life
brings you not only as a spiritual lesson or gift, but also as a spiritual
parent. Yes, all that life brings, every person and experience, is a spiritual parent, helping to grow you in the matters of spirit. See your life
being "raised" by everything you encounter. This is what it means to be
a child of God.

Make a vow to bring more play into your family life, whether it
involves parents, siblings, children, or grandchildren. Allow it to transform family events, holidays, and get-togethers into an absurd theater
for spiritual growth. Life is already absurd, anyway. Why not go the
next step and stretch it into the trickster realm? Bring the arms of the
cross into the lives of those to whom you are most closely related.

## ✦ DIRECTIVE: THE FAMILY SIGNATURE

Purchase an oversized pen or pencil and have the whole family participate in the following exercise. Have everyone hold onto the big pen or
pencil, and together, all family members are to sign the family name on
the inside of the family Bible. Consider this the family signature. In the
future, when an important family decision is made, get out the pen and
ritualize the decision by signing the family name.

### Considerations

- Consider having different family pens—one for signing holiday
  cards, another for legal matters, still another for making special
  commitments, and so forth.
- In the manner described, use the big pen or pencil to write the
  family name inside each family member's Bible.
- Sign the family name on an outside corner of the house.
- Make a family prayer and sign the family name to it. Keep this in
  a special place. Read it at special family gatherings.
- Create a ritual with candles and music to be performed whenever
  the family name is signed.

## ✦ DIRECTIVE: ADOPT A SAINT

Have a family meeting and agree to fictionally "adopt" a saint. Choose
any saint who has written a book or has been the subject of a book written by someone else. Set aside a time each evening for family members
to take turns reading from one of these books. Call this saint an aunt or
uncle. Before each evening's reading session, establish a family ritual of
having someone say, "What has Uncle John or Aunt Catherine sent us
tonight?" Then pretend that what is read was written especially for your
family. Try to read all of your saint's written works. Notice when the
saint really does begin to feel like a member of the family.

## Considerations

- Send a birthday card on the saint's day. If there isn't a designated day to celebrate the saint, choose one yourself. Address it to your home.
- Build an altar to your saint. Make sure that all the books by or about the saint are in its vicinity.
- Make sure something silly is included in this altar. Discuss what might make the saint laugh.
- Place a homemade halo over the altar. Invite each family member to stand under it at least once a week.
- Make a prayer to have a dream about the saint. Celebrate the day anyone dreams of the saint. Write down the dream and place it on the altar.

## ✦ Directive: On Not Listening

Choose a time when everyone in the family can eat dinner together. At this meal everyone must try, to the best of their abilities, to not listen and not pay attention to anyone else. Each person must say at least one nonsense sentence about spirituality. For example, "God enjoys swallowing colors that sing too loudly." After the meal, have a discussion to find out if everyone heard any particular words, in spite of each person's efforts to not hear anyone else.

## Considerations

- Try playing some background music to help keep you distracted. Try music that no one likes or music that no one has heard before, or take turns playing each person's favorite music. Experiment!
- See who is best at not listening. Have them teach the others how to be more effective at it.
- Find out if one word is noticed more often than others.
- Have each person repeat their one sentence at three different times during the meal. Say it differently each time.
- Ask your family members to spend some time preparing their nonsensical spiritual statements. Then give them permission to change the statements at the last moment.

## ✦ DIRECTIVE: MYSTERY CARDS

Provide each family member with several dollars to be used exclusively to buy picture postcards, one for each member of the family. These post-cards must be purchased in secret, and no family member should show anyone else what they bought. Each person should then send cards to the other family members. Everyone should disguise his or her writing or type the message, if possible, so nobody's handwriting can be recognized. Each card should say nothing more than, "May the spirit be with you." Discover whether family members can guess who sent each cards. No one should tell which cards they sent. This is to remain a family mystery.

### Considerations

- Send mystery gifts to the family.
- Send the family a stone with one word written on it.
- Send a Bible that is published in a foreign language. Try reading it aloud, making up how you think the words should sound.
- Send the family a leaf that has spent a week inside a Bible.
- Send a fictitious letter from God.

## ✦ DIRECTIVE: HOLY SILENCE

Obtain an audio recorder. Have each family member do the following. Set the machine on "record" and imagine saying a prayer for everyone in the family, but do not say anything aloud. Remain silent, saying the prayers only in your mind. Record for no longer than three minutes. After all family members have recorded their prayers, gather the family together and play the silent tape. Turn the volume to medium loudness, as if there were something to hear. Remain silent and listen. Imagine what each person prayed.

### Considerations

- Consider this practice to be a way to amplify silent prayer.
- Invite others to join your family in this kind of empowered, silent praying.

- Silently pray for someone in your family who is away, and send them the silent prayer.
- Before performing the exercise, prepare the tape for one week: Sprinkle it with blessed water, keep it inside the family Bible, hold it over your heart, sing to it, and so forth. After it has been blessed, record the silent prayers.
- Date all the recorded silent prayers and keep them in a special place. See it as a family tower of prayer.

## ✦ DIRECTIVE: SECRET BLESSINGS

The parents (or parent) of the family are to go to the backyard or the nearest park and choose a leaf for every family member. They should choose leaves that remind them of each individual. After the family members receive their leaves, tell them to carry the leaf with them during the following day. At the end of the day, have the children give the leaves back. Place them in a jar and store them somewhere safe.

Once a week, pull out the jar and let everyone look at the leaves. Over time, when the leaves become dry, brittle, and begin breaking apart, crumble the leaves into a powder and thoroughly mix it. Next, without telling anyone, sprinkle a tiny amount of this powder into each child's shoes while they are sleeping. Make a blessing for each child as you do this. One year later, tell each child what you did.

### Considerations

- When you tell the children about the blessing you made for them, say that you will do this once a year. Call that the family blessing day.
- Ask the children to do this for you and your spouse. They are to collect the leaves and make a blessing for you.
- Save a little powder from everyone's shoes and mix it together. Make this into a whole family blessing.
- When someone is sick or facing a challenge, make a special family blessing for them using the dried leaves.
- Make family blessings for others in need without letting them

know they are being blessed. Bless your neighborhood, school, community, and the world.

## ✦ DIRECTIVE: THE SECRET WORD

Count the number of family members living in your present household. Choose the same number of letters from the alphabet by having each family member choose one letter and write it on a small piece of paper. The family must then meet and arrange these letters into a secret family word. The family must decide whether or not they will tell anyone outside the family about this secret word.

### *Considerations*
- When making the family signature, add this secret word to the signature.
- Send a holiday card to this word, using your home address.
- When the family gets the giggles together, someone should say the word.
- When praying together, use the word before saying "Amen."
- Include the word on the family altar.
- Write the word on top of John 3:16 inside your Bible.

## ✦ DIRECTIVE: SPIRITUAL MENTORING

Make a list of the ten holy people from the past or present who have been most influential in capturing your imagination, inspiring your life, and contributing to your spiritual development. This list may include people you know personally as well as people you have never met, as long as their ideas or presence have influenced your life.

For each name on your list, write a sentence that captures how this person contributed to your spiritual life. Next, in each of these sentences, circle the one word that you feel is most representative of and most resonant with the intended meaning of the sentence.

Now, write one paragraph using only the words you circled in each sentence. This paragraph should represent your best effort to summarize what you believe is the meaning of your life. Read this paragraph to someone in your family once a day for the next three days. Then wrap it up neatly and place it in the freezer.

The next time you're feeling as if you don't understand the meaning of your life, go to your freezer, remove your paragraph, and pretend to allow it to thaw. When it's thawed, read it to someone in your family once a day for the next three days. Then wrap it up again neatly and return it to the freezer.

## Considerations

- Make another list of the silliest and most absurd people you have known or heard about. Repeat the process with the names of these people and their "silly wisdom." Consider the silly wisdom to be as holy as the spiritual wisdom.
- Think of your freezer as a shrine of wisdom.
- Imagine that each thawing and refreezing deepens the wisdom of the words you have read.
- Imagine that your inner being contains a deep freezer in which unspoken wisdom is stored. Every time you thaw the paragraphs in your kitchen freezer, believe you are also thawing and accessing wisdom from the depths of your inner being.
- From time to time you may see a movie, read a book, meet a person, have a dream, or undergo an experience that deeply influences your life. Collect ten of these special moments and repeat the procedure just described, creating ten sentences and selecting ten key words from them. Write a second paragraph about the meaning of life and add it to your freezer. Thaw this paragraph out and read it to someone in your family when you feel that you are in need of adding more meaning to your life.

## ✦ DIRECTIVE: TREE RELATIVES

Take the whole family to the park nearest to where you live. Choose a tree everyone feels a connection with. If you can't find such a tree, try another park. Once you find a special tree, visit it as often as possible.

Pick up any trash you find around it, touch it, and say kind words to it. Think about this tree during the week. When it feels as though it is part of your family, take a picture of it. Give your tree a name and hang an enlarged photograph of the tree in a special place in your home. Include an acknowledgment of the tree in all family holidays and celebrations.

## Considerations

- Find other trees to make a relationship with and build an extended family network. Over time you will build up a family forest. Keep a list of names of all of the trees.
- Adopt a state park or national forest without telling anyone you have done so. Visit this place once a year and prepare a special ritual and feast for the annual homecoming.
- Build a scrapbook of tree photographs, names, and remembered moments from special homecomings.
- Consider branching out and adopting a shrub or other plant. Expand your family.
- Select a saint to watch over your tree relatives. Pray to this saint and ask it to take care of all trees.

## ✦ DIRECTIVE: PET'S VACATION

This assignment is for families with a dog. (If you don't have a dog, consider getting one. If you do, wait a year and then try this one.)

Plan a weekend or week-long family trip for your pet. Think about where your pet might like to visit. What itinerary can the family plan? Plan for special meals, games, and surprises. Include a shamanic ritual for the pet. Perhaps read it a Bible verse, but translate it into barking as you read from the Bible. Take photographs and create a scrapbook of the trip. Make this a special vacation no one in the family will ever forget!

## Considerations

- Encourage other dog lovers to take trips with their own dogs. Talk about it with your neighbors and friends.

- Organize a caravan of several families and take all of your dogs on a special trip.
- Send postcards from your dog to the pets of friends.
- Discuss all the places in the world your dog might enjoy visiting if you had the funding to take it anywhere. Go there in your imagination.
- Send a thank you card to your dog for bringing you along on its trip. Tell your dog what it meant to you and recall the special moments you will always remember.

## CONCLUDING THOUGHTS

No person is an island. We all live in a social ecology of relationships whether they are physically visible or not. The Christian shaman cultivates a remembrance that we are always individuals-in-relationship. More specifically, there is no such thing as an individual because we cannot be out of relationship. The powerful implication of this relational view is that any perceived change of an individual is actually a change of a relationship. This brings new meaning to the adages, "change yourself if you hope to change others" and "improve yourself in order to improve the world." Bringing trickster wisdom and absurdity into your family life may be the most powerful means of changing the planet. The bigger the relational unit that is immersed in shamanic transformation, the more powerful the consequences on the greater ecology. To change and evolve our culture, begin by changing and evolving your family life. Do so with a deep commitment to being lighthearted.

# THE LOST EPISTLE
## On Becoming a
## Christian Shaman

*And then it was found, lost again, and found again and again.*

INSCRIPTION FROM THE LOST EPISTLE

Sometime during the early 1950s an Oxford debate team enrolled in a college course on the "archaeology of debate." The course addressed the topic of how archaeological remains could provide evidence that ancient people practiced the art of debate. The course was taught by an eccentric scholar who arranged funding for the debate team to go on a field trip to the Middle East. There they discovered a treasure chest with an ancient fortune cookie inside. They subsequently argued over whether or not to open it. Finally a compromise was made. They would open it twenty-five years from the time of its discovery, on December 25 of that year. The group privately agreed to call that day the beginning of a more fortunate age. They then proceeded to celebrate with a bottle of wine, joking the night away and forgetting whatever concerns they had about whether or not to open the fortune cookie.

The scholars waited twenty-five years and finally opened the fortune cookie, thereby celebrating the initiation of a new age, a more fortunate age. But the fortune cookie held no words. It simply contained a phone number. They called the number and to their surprise, an answering machine gave them directions to a library located in a small village south of the equator. The message ended with the instruction, "When you get to the library, check the dictionary definition of the word *fortune*." When they finally arrived at the remote library, they marched straight to the reference room, where they saw the largest dictionary they had ever seen in their lives. Climbing up a ladder to a control tower that permitted them to turn the dictionary's pages with an elaborate set of extremely long mechanical arms, they worked their way toward the correct page. One of the definitions was stated simply and clearly:

*Fortune: an unknown and unpredictable phenomenon that leads to a favorable outcome.*

That was the end of their journey. They had waited twenty-five years to take off on a journey that led them to the definition of *fortune*. They debated whether or not they had been fortunate. Reaching no agreement, they returned to their lives, but none of them ever stopped thinking about the meaning of the word *fortune*.

Then, one of the former Oxford debate team members decided to do something he had never done before in his life. He prayed. Not just any prayer, but a prayer requesting guidance about the meaning of a single word. In front of a lit, white candle, he got on his knees and sincerely spoke this prayer:

*Dear God,*
   *What is the meaning of "fortune?"*

*Thank you.*
*Amen*

That evening, the intellectual had a vision that changed the course of his life. He stepped fully into the heavens of creative imagination, where he was handed an old epistle wrapped with a leather band. The title, which he had to translate from Latin, was *The Lost Epistle*. We are fortunate that he specified in his will that the lessons of this epistle be shared with the world if—and only if—a book entitled *Shamanic Christianity* ever were to appear in print. Honoring his request, we end with this historical sharing of lost words about the lost teachings and the lost directives:

*My Dear Christian Shamans,*

   *My heart is deeply touched that you have been introduced to the lost teachings and the lost directives. They will help you become, unbecome, and become again in all matters concerning the spirit of our Lord, whose Kingdom has come and gone and come again. Let me leave you with some final advice and several doses of uncommon wisdom. Without further ado, I present this as a Christian shaman's final list. Consider it an enumeration of ideas, none fully developed, but presented with hope that they may become seeds to sprout into whatever forms fit your unique way of knowing and being in the world. These are the lessons taught by* The Lost Epistle.

1. Know that most of today's so-called shamans, spiritual teachers, and elders have lost their way. Somewhere along the path they lost their childlike nature. You will recognize them by their overseriousness, their judgmental pronouncements, and their literalism. Their words will reflect fundamentalism in all sizes and shapes. Do not listen to them. Instead, try to play with them, hoping that the disturbance created by your presence might awaken what they have forgotten.

2. Some will say that you, a shaman, must be seriously concerned about spiritual protection. Be careful not to become too preoccupied with protection. The rituals of protection too easily call forth the dichotomy of good and evil, giving evil more weight than it deserves. We feed evil when we are too serious about it. Stand in the light, feel the love, and then get downright silly. That's a triple whammy: Evil hates light, love, and laughter. It will slip in only if one of those three guardians is not present. Of these three, perhaps the most powerful protection is the laughter

of a child. Open your spiritual valves with shaking childish merriment. Then you will be ready to do God's work.

3. There are times to get serious: The experiences of ecstatic energy and visionary rapture will take your breath away. Be serious about them, but only during the moments in which they occur. Afterward, return to levity. Forget forging the truth onto iron. Instead, be available time and time again for the spirit to catch you, ride you, and fly you anew.

4. There are four sacred corners of the Christian shaman's mystical cross:

- The ecstatic life force (or Holy Ghost power, kundalini, chi)
- Spiritual vision
- Creative expression
- Absurd experience

   Never stay stuck in any one corner. Keep moving from one corner to another. This is the road you must stay on, and you must keep moving on it. The road is circular. It deepens, broadens, and heightens with each cycle you traverse. It is this virtuous cycle that makes the shaman.

5. Here are four truths to go along with the four corners of the cross:

   *No shake, no shaman.* You must learn to shake with joy and spiritual fervor.

   *No music, no shaman.* God talks primarily through music and rhythm.

   *No vision, no shaman.* I'm not talking about psychological dreams, but spirit-infused perception, which comes either through sacred dream or waking vision.

   *No absurdity, no shaman.* There is no such thing as a serious shaman; there are only laughing shamans and serious shams.

6. The Christian shaman loves all the religions of the world and feels free to play with them in a trickster way. This includes the unwritten religions and the unspoken traditions.

7. Be your own missionary. Convert one other person to shamanic

Christianity so you have a playmate. Two's a sandlot; three's a party.

8. There is one other time to be serious. Be very, very serious about your prayer life. Pray religiously and wholeheartedly. You have to show God and the deepest parts of your being that you are sincere about this.

9. Do more than pray: Act out your desire to make a connection with spirit. Without the enactment of ritual—performing the suggested rituals and conducting the lost directives—it will be more difficult to get inside the mystical gates. Few will enter the gate, because few have the divine madness required to stretch the dichotomies as far as they need to be stretched. Remember, the cross must be stretched to open the gate to the mysteries.

10. One word sums it all up: *love*. This is all about love, and only love. It is never about having power, being special, or getting magic. Love is the God we serve, wild, complete love in all possible forms and manifestations. Love is the Mystical Christ, the Holy Mother, and all the saints. The Big Love is the name of the shaman's worship. Surrender to it, and it will set you free.

11. Say, "Thank you" or "Thank you, Jesus" or "Thank you, Mary" or "Thank you, Holy Mother" or "Thank you, Holy Father" or "Thank you, Lord" over and over throughout each day and night. This is your mantra and secret saying. Thank the Lord for every breath and every experience. When you pray for guidance and don't get a big vision, say "Thank you."

12. Always remember that there is really no such thing as an individual. No one lives outside of relationship—relationships with significant others, community, and the natural world. What you may regard as "work on self" is always "work with others." The opposite is also true: Your work with others and the outside world simultaneously becomes work on your internal nature. The outer and inner are mirrored and aligned.

I leave you now with a final directive, a graduation present as you continue your approach toward the never-ending mysteries:

When you feel it is time to graduate into the higher mysteries, make a paper cross that you design, cut out, color, and adorn with symbols that are meaningful to you. Wrap this cross with green yarn that looks like a coiled snake. Tape the yarn onto the cross. Before bedtime, anoint the cross with a drop of perfume and bless it with a prayer. Ask it to help you open the next door. Regard it as a shamanic key. Now tape the specially prepared and blessed cross to the bottom of your spine. Sleep through the night with it. Repeat every night for at least a month as you prepare to receive new direction from the dreamtime.

Now let us pray together, asking that we may all persevere and move into each day with the fullest possible expression of shamanic Christianity.

*Dear Lord,*

*We surrender to your holy blessings, holy gifts, holy teachings, holy visions, and holy madness. We devote ourselves to being wise and foolish, all in your name. We submit wholeheartedly to your divine love, a love that never judges others, but embraces everyone as a reflection of you and a reflection of our own being. Help us to be good and kind. Help us to be servants of play, masters of ignorance, and instigators of shaking truth. Reduce us to nothing, so we may revel in all things. Fill us with your light so that we may be strong, in order to hold and release all that comes our way. Help us to stretch both vertically and horizontally.*

*In these ways, help us become a walking cross, with arms that fully embrace life and a body that is both high in the spiritual sky and deeply rooted in the Earth. Bless us, so that we may remain children of your spirit. Help us to honor all our parents, all the ancestors who were, are, and will be. In all of these things, we celebrate and rejoice through your name and your presence. We ask to be moved out of the way, so that we are instruments for your divine play. We ask that your will be done in and through us. Thank you, Jesus. Thank you, Lord. From the bottom of my heart, thank you, thank you, thank you. Amen. Amen. Amen.*

# APPENDIX
*Message for the*
*World Worrier*

Consider the fact that there are other people all around the world who find they worry too much and don't know why they worry more than other people. Assume that God has become so worried about the delicate balance of life on Earth that a global alarm has gone off. God has chosen some people to worry and ask themselves why they worry so much. One by one, these people are realizing that their responsibility is to spread the worry around, so we will do what must be done before it is too late.

# ABOUT THE AUTHOR

Bradford Keeney, Ph.D., has carried out one of the broadest and most intense field studies of global shamanism in history. As distinguished scholar of cultural studies for the Ringing Rocks Foundation, he led expeditions throughout the world to study cultural healing practices, and he edited the critically acclaimed book series *Profiles of Healing*, a ten-volume encyclopedia of the world's healing practices. He is the subject of the book *American Shaman: An Odyssey of Global Healing Traditions* written by Jeffrey Kottler and Jon Carlson, which was awarded a Best Spiritual Book award by *Spirituality and Health Magazine* in 2004.

Keeney is accepted as an elder shaman and teacher in numerous cultures throughout the world, including the Guarani Indians of lower basin Amazonia, the Zulu sangoma community, the elder Shakers of St. Vincent, diverse folk healers of Brazil, the Balians of Bali, and by practitioners of the Japanese tradition of *seiki jutsu*. He is regarded as a *n/om kxao* (owner of spiritual power) by the Bushmen of Namibia and Botswana.

Keeney has also worked at some of the most respected psychotherapy centers in the United States, including the Ackerman Institute in New York City, the Karl Menninger Center in Topeka, and the Philadelphia Child Guidance Clinic, and he served as director of several family therapy doctoral programs. His creative approach to psychotherapy is presented in the clinical videotape series *Brief Therapy Inside Out,* produced by Zeig, Tucker & Thiesen. A clinical member, approved supervisor, and fellow of the American Association for Marriage and Family Therapy as well as advisory board member of the National Academy for Certified Family Therapists, he has presented training programs, workshops, and keynote addresses throughout the world and has appeared on numerous radio and television programs.

The author of several classics in the field of family therapy, including *Aesthetics of Change, Mind in Therapy,* and *Improvisational Therapy,* he has also written numerous titles for the popular press, such as *Everyday Soul, The Energy Break, Shaking Out the Spirits, Crazy Wisdom Tales, Bushman Shaman: Awakening the Spirit through Ecstatic Dance,* and *Milton H. Erickson, M.D.: An American Healer* (with Betty Alice Erickson). He is also an improvisational jazz pianist and ecstatic drummer and has toured the world from New York City to Rio de Janeiro, including a special performance with jazz guitarist Al Di Meola at the Miami Arena.

# BOOKS OF RELATED INTEREST

**Bushman Shaman**
*Awakening the Spirit through Ecstatic Dance*
by Bradford Keeney

**Shamanic Experience**
*A Practical Guide to Psychic Powers*
by Kenneth Meadows

**Hildegard von Bingen's Mystical Visions**
*Translated from Scivias*
by Bruce Hozeski

**Passion for Creation**
*The Earth-Honoring Spirituality of Meister Eckhart*
by Matthew Fox

**A New Reformation**
*Creation Spirituality and the Transformation of Christianity*
by Matthew Fox

**Gnostic Philosophy**
*From Ancient Persia to Modern Times*
by Tobias Churton

**Zulu Shaman**
*Dreams, Prophecies, and Mysteries*
Vusamazulu Credo Mutwa
Edited by Stephen Larsen

**Vodou Shaman**
*The Haitian Way of Healing and Power*
by Ross Heaven

**Inner Traditions • Bear & Company**
P.O. Box 388
Rochester, VT 05767
1-800-246-8648
www.InnerTraditions.com

Or contact your local bookseller